The Case for
Universal Basic Income

T0044928

Louise Haagh

———————

The Case for Universal Basic Income

polity

First published in 2019 by Polity Press

Polity Press
65 Bridge Street
Cambridge CB2 1UR, UK

Polity Press
101 Station Landing
Suite 300
Medford, MA 02155, USA

ISBN-13: 978-1-5095-2295-8
ISBN-13: 978-1-5095-2296-5 (pb)

A catalogue record for this book is available from the British Library.

Library of Congress Cataloging-in-Publication Data

Names: Haagh, Louise, 1967- author.
Title: The case for universal basic income / Louise Haagh.
Description: Medford, MA : Polity, 2019. | Series: The Case for | Includes
    bibliographical references and index.
Identifiers: LCCN 2018029800 (print) | LCCN 2018035479 (ebook) | ISBN
    9781509522996 (Epub) | ISBN 9781509522958 (hardback) | ISBN
9781509522965
    (paperback)
Subjects: LCSH: Income distribution. | Welfare state. | Distributive justice.
    | BISAC: POLITICAL SCIENCE / Public Policy / Economic Policy.
Classification: LCC HB523 (ebook) | LCC HB523 .H33 2019 (print) | DDC
    331.2/36--dc23
LC record available at https://lccn.loc.gov/2018029800

Typeset in 11 on 15 Sabon by Servis Filmsetting Ltd, Stockport, Cheshire
Printed and bound in Great Britain by T.J. International Ltd.

For further information on Polity, visit our website: politybooks.com

Contents

Tables and Figures

Tables and Figures

Acknowledgements

This book is the product of many people's support. I especially want to thank the editorial team at Polity Press, above all George Owers, for his many wise suggestions, Ian Tuttle, for his incisive scrutiny, Julia Davies, for expertly overseeing the process of writing, and several anonymous referees, who commented generously on previous versions of this manuscript. All errors are mine.

The thoughts in these pages emerge from a diverse set of influences. Growing up in an egalitarian Nordic culture informed my perspective on substantive democracy. My work with local union leaders in Chile helped me understand the importance of local representation. Studying labour relations in East Asia and social protection in Latin America strengthened my sense of the importance of stable economic structures in human development.

Acknowledgements

I became interested in basic income in 2002, and from the beginning perceived its key role in democratising the welfare state. After 2008 I became more preoccupied with the study of development in high income countries, a time coinciding with sustained crisis in the public sector, reinforcing in my mind a need to set basic income in a broader context of rethinking the civilisation project.

I am heavily indebted to the British Academy, the Nuffield Foundation, The Leverhulme Trust, and the Economic and Social Research Council, for funding research and fellowships over the years. I acknowledge the influence of my early mentors, Alan Angell, Laurence Whitehead, Samuel Valenzuela, and Gabriel Palma and Ha-Joon Chang.

My engagement with basic income debate is almost wholly down to the community of scholars and activists involved in the Basic Income Earth Network, including – in order that I met them - Eduardo Suplicy, Philippe van Parijs, Guy Standing, Rubén lo Vuolo, Lena Lavinas, Karl Widerquist, Jurgen de Wispelaere, David Cassasas, Ingrid van Niekerk, Michael Howard, Almaz Zelleke, Claus Offe, Annie Miller, Malcolm Torry, and Sarath Dawala, to mention only some of the names.

I am grateful to my colleagues who have hosted recent debates on basic income, including

Acknowledgements

BIEN Denmark, and in Britain, Marc Winn of the Dandelion Foundation, Anthony Painter of the Royal Society of Arts, and Lord Liddle, Jeff McMahan and Peer Zumbansen, for workshops at Westminster, Corpus Christi, and King's College, during 2017-2018. I have learnt a great deal from recent engagements with international organisations, in particular the groups led by Gilda Farrell within the Council of Europe, and by Christine Brown, within the World Health Organisation. My deepest gratitude extends to my close friends and family, including Ed, Mille, Neil, Ato, and Teddy. I dedicate this book to my sons, and to the memory of my mother and grandparents, whose guidance remain my inspiration today.

For Ato and Teddy, and in memory of Birte,
Dagmar, Rigmor and Albert
With love and gratitude

1

Basic Income in Time

A Democratic Humanist Case for Basic Income Reform

The idea of a basic income – to give all residents a modest regular income grant that is not dependent on means-tests or work requirement – has caught the attention of policy-makers and social activists across the globe. The proposal has been around for a long time. English radicals put forward a version in late eighteenth-century England: Thomas Spence as a dividend from communally owned land,[1] and Thomas Paine as a payment from land rent to make up for the private appropriation of the commons with 'a right, not a charity'.[2] Basic income initiatives have appeared since in different guises. One variety discussed in the United States in the 1970s involved simplifying and reducing welfare services in favour of alleviating poverty.[3] Basic income has recently resurfaced in Europe with a referendum in Switzerland in 2016, and in 2017 the Finnish government introduced a two-year official experiment investigating a partial form of this policy by lifting conditions on income support. Municipalities in a series of other countries, including the Netherlands, Denmark, France and Spain, have launched similar pilots. However, the idea remains controversial, with a British parliamentary enquiry concluding that the citizens' income is 'not the solution to welfare state problems'.[4] If distributing money on a regular and life-long basis to everyone is desirable, why is the plan thought so controversial? And why has the idea not been pursued until now?

The first thing to note about basic income is the wide spectrum of support the scheme enjoys. Endorsements from varying ideological schools share a common claim from which this book takes its departure: whatever form you might think society ought to take, whether you support an enterprise or a cooperative economy, first, a society of individuals functioning on their own and together needs to come into being. Incorporation is a foundation for civilization, the market, human development, social equality and democracy. Postwar welfare states made strides in social incorporation, but their foundations were weak. Containing working-age adults within society was too reliant on one institution: the employment contract. This contract form lacked an independent underpinning. The result was bureaucratic intrusion into individuals' decisions in the course of administering rights to subsistence. States which supported individuals' freedom through health and schooling took it away in the marketplace. As employment became more precarious, the coercive implications of the lack of independent material security for all have only got worse.

Hence, this book argues for basic income as part of democratic reconstruction at a juncture of global crisis in governance. Capacity in the state and society for governing humanely – with regard for each individual's trajectory – depends on the polity first acting in a society-constitutive role, defined as building individual capabilities, on the one hand, and cooperative capabilities, on the other. The case for basic income I make is therefore a case for democratic equality grounded in equal interests humans have in existential security. Basic income can be viewed in this context as a pivoting transformation, a form of institution-building that, by stabilizing the individual economy, can ignite other positive changes. The political scientist Bremner described states that gain strength and stability within the international system by not being reliant on any one other state as pivoting states.[5] Basic income is grounding in a broader as well as deeper sense, in this case as stabilizing the lives of all individuals makes for more resilient communities, sub-nationally, nationally and globally. A civilized social order depends on not just strategic players but all constituent units enjoying a foundation of existential security.

Basic income may contribute to more stable and democratic societies in a number of ways: first, stabilizing the human condition by giving everyone some existential security, may support genuinely motivated activity, and unitary senses of self. Income support systems based in means- and behaviour testing that now predominate make crises in individuals' lives a source of altered social status and therefore permanent. Currently, individuals in good jobs rely entirely on those jobs. Individuals on income support fear losing it. Neither group benefits from the status exclusions that define their mutual relation and station. Income security structures set up this way subvert the effect of other life-long guarantees, as represented in universal health. By instead converting divisive and unstable income security to unconditional communal property, basic income entails a stand against both moral and material destitution, helping to prevent individuals having to lean on one dependent relation or institution, and then another, angling for, yet never achieving, a sense of basic independence. The way that establishing or losing control over one's life hangs on a form of constant support was understood by many who have supported basic income, including the postwar British economist James Meade, who used a path diagram of individual life histories to understand the progression of economic inequalities, and the British political philosopher Brian Barry, who saw basic income as a way to abate cumulative disadvantage.[6] Basic income, however, also sets out a different way of thinking about the form of the most important institutions shaping the human life course. Economic security surveys show that mental states are positively affected by enjoying at once stability in education, external income security, and employment.[7] In this context, the image of the pivot represents the way an individual standing upright – enjoying independence of self – is someone who has support from many sources, yet has reason to feel confident her basic status is unaffected by any one source of support.[8]

Second, by extension, basic income may contribute to greater stability and equality in social relations, thus generating a basis for cooperation in society. As basic income extends to all citizens – as well as a whole life – it enables a sense of community, whilst underpinning systems that respond to variation in needs.

Finally, at the level of systems, basic income may generate a stable monetary foundation on which other public development and social policies can build and support each other's effects. Today, across Europe's mature welfare states, emerging gaps in benefit access have been identified by public service providers – such as head-teachers, and leading medical professionals – as a chief cause of stunted growth and relative child poverty.[9] A range of studies have documented adverse health impacts of anticipating benefit status assessment within different European countries,[10] including in Norway,[11] Denmark[12] and Britain,[13] despite different systems of application.

The Marmot review into health inequality in Britain identified barriers to income benefit access as a cause of grave concern,[14] whilst also guarding against simply targeting specific groups, and promoting instead cross-sectoral approaches.[15] However, what in practice does better policy coherence for human development require? On what does it rest? How is income insecurity a health issue of all groups in society? In this book I argue that insecurity in society is epidemiological. Not only does insecurity that affects some groups more visibly have shared structural roots. In addition, those secure today see in others their own insecurity tomorrow. Fear within social groups deepens division between them, and thus breaks down societal trust in immeasurable ways. In this context, I argue that a basic income is civilizing. Like basic health and schooling, basic income is a form of hybrid property in that it gives individuals rights while also belonging to and strengthening society. By weaving basic security into the fabric of society, basic income is a rising tide, lifting all boats, whilst bringing those stranded into common waters. At the same time, the way basic income is pitched in relation to other services in society and development policies matters. Deregulatory policies since the 1980s, culminating in the global crisis of 2008, and ensuing public austerity, and rising inequality, cast civil society as the marketplace, and social services as a last resort. In this altered context, misrepresentations of basic income as a singular distributive measure, including through usurpation by populist tides and narrow polemics, become more likely. Hence, despite having greater moral appeal in conditions of rising inequality, basic income may itself be both less likely and effective in this context. The upshot of this equality paradox is to place conditions *for* basic income in the foreground: the universal welfare state needs basic income – but basic income also needs the universal welfare state and the solidarity and regulatory systems on which it has rested.

On that basis, I set a civic model of basic income apart from two other contemporary models, an adapted version of basic income, such as the Negative Income Tax, which in effect targets the poor; and a libertarian model which favours direct transaction and hence competition in governing social life, normatively and practically. To further clarify how basic income forms part of wider debates about contemporary society, I will draw out why the balance between competition and cooperation in the economy matters. The Danish political scientist Ove Pedersen has argued that the emergence since the 1980s of so-called competition states – defined by a new imperative to ensure all units in the economy are used to advance economic efficiency – occurred surreptitiously, without being fully reasoned for.[16] On the other hand, states today are only to varying and often a diminishing degree in charge of the process. Growing reliance on high-interest borrowing to fund public services,[17] and – in Europe – tight restrictions on public budgets to help resolve the private finance crisis,[18] are symptomatic of a weakened regulatory and fiscal state. Hence, a competition economy has grown as a force in its own right to the extent that public choice-sets are narrowed. Thus, if basic income always has been closely bound up with the development of the welfare state, today marks a watershed moment, at which rethinking the connection is critical. What this means of course has many elements, but in this book I focus on meanings I link with institutions of human development.

Accordingly, in this chapter I set out how the human development democratic case for basic income I make is distinctive and relevant today. I first address elementary confusions, and how the democratic and human development case can help answer them. Next, I briefly trace how this builds on the human development approach, and relates with other approaches, by explicitly connecting the case for basic income with addressing flaws in the postwar welfare state, as well as in the contemporary global competition economy. In the remaining chapters, I elaborate how the human development and democratic case is connected with freedom and justice, and with constructing governance capabilities in the state and society.

Just a Fad?

Because a basic income is paid regularly, without means-test or behaviour conditionalities, and to individuals, it is often compared with the public pension or child allowances. These provisions in turn are sometimes considered routes to basic income reform. In this context, the most common concern about basic income is that it is paid to all, including working-age adults and those with money and property. The case for doing so, however, is usually stated in terms of rights: the social theorist of the 1960s Richard Titmuss's famous saying that 'separate discriminatory services for poor people have always tended to be poor quality services'[19] applies with equal force to income security. Like Paine, Titmuss wanted to put an end to charity, 'to abolish the need to be moral'.[20] An evident rationale for at least a certain basic level of permanent income security for all is that this guards against income security provision being used coercively, or dwindling into pithy handouts. An obvious case against basic income, on the other hand, is that it does not exist. If we have done alright until now without a basic income, why don't we focus on improving things that have been shown to work? Can we really afford another costly experiment?

Yet, before we dismiss basic income as just a fad, we need to consider a number of basic points.

First, the idea of unconditional rights to monetary security may be thought neither new nor radical when we survey the cross-cutting support the scheme has enjoyed. For people on the left, support for this proposition by market liberals, from Friedrich Hayek[21] in the 1940s, to Milton Friedman in the 1960s, and Charles Murray[22] and founder of Facebook, Mark Zuckerberg,[23] today, all protagonists of privatizing welfare, or of reducing the role of the state, is a concern. Yet, support for basic income has also been strong among left liberals and critical theorists, from Bertrand Russell[24] in the 1930s, to the German social theorist Claus Offe[25] in the 1980s. In their own way, all understood that modern states had failed to secure the basic independent status of citizens.

Second, basic income is already an electorally viable idea, notionally supported by half of the population of Europe.[26] Although populations in high-welfare states are more sceptical, we should not assume this is connected with rejection of universal rights to security. The couching by the European Social Survey of basic income as a 'replacement' of other benefits may have contributed to a misperception that eradication of a whole class of benefits, rather than some of their cost, is at stake.[27] The campaign for the 2016 referendum in Switzerland which basic income proponents lost – with only 23% in favour – had quoted a higher level of basic income than commonly discussed.[28] Moreover, scepticism about basic income among societal actors may be tied to the way the proposal is sometimes connected with futuristic projections about artificial intelligence (AI) and a workless society[29] rather than practical problems we face right now.

Finally, since libertarian proposals for basic income linked with a smaller role for the state are the best known, many people understand basic income as a transfer to compensate other forms of exclusion. This drives other common misunderstandings, including the idea that basic income will replace wage incomes or employment, that it is connected with 'an ideology of idleness',[30] or that it is essentially a way to address poverty.

Basic Income, Human Development and Citizen Equality

To understand how basic income is relevant for civilization and democracy, we need to ask a different set of questions: rather than being a displacement of the welfare state, formal employment or cooperation, is basic income important or even essential in some form, to make those work? If we are to make that case, on what grounds would it be? If basic income is clearly not the answer to all of the problems of the welfare state, can we afford *not* to implement a right to basic monetary security?

When we conceive of basic income in practical terms as a condition of modern society, its constitutive role as an enabler of human development and social cooperation comes into view. Among the many practical reasons for basic income, the most general is how basic income fills a gap in the infrastructure of modern democracies and economies. In this book, I tie a democratic and governance case for basic income to a case for human development in the understanding that the viability of economic and political systems depends on developmental trajectories of individuals succeeding. Basic income is, along with other institutions of social incorporation, essential to make this happen.

The debates and problems we have today grew out of the ideological wars of the 1960s, between those wanting to improve welfare, like Titmuss, and those wanting to minimize it, like Friedman. In this battle of ideas, the school of market economics could draw on the flaws in the postwar project, and did so successfully. The meaning of Titmuss's comment about separate services is pertinent here. At stake in targeting services to the poor is not just stigma, the identification of 'faults in the individual' rather than 'faults in society', and 'treating applicants as supplicants'.[31] Titmuss foresaw the roots of this form of welfare in inequality. He anticipated consequently the damaging effects that an ideology of public austerity – defined as the notion that public spending is waste and must be cut to favour the market[32] – would have. Austerity as an ideology of the market applied to the public is essentially about breaking down *public* costs into the smallest part – for everything that is spent must have a justified 'cause', not because this system saves for society as whole, but because the public sector is defined in narrow assistentialist terms. As Titmuss put it so aptly, conservative discourse about welfare is above all concerned with 'unidentifiable causality', defined as 'waste'.[33] The shared form of basic income contests this morality and definition of waste as 'non-authorized' spend, by suggesting that the attempt to identify causality, specifically the exact reasons people choose or not to work particular jobs, with the intent to reduce basic income security, also cannot be done without waste and coercion. Rather, security by definition is shared, and reduces overall waste by permitting a holistic programme of social and human development.

How does the human development and democratic case for basic income add to familiar arguments? In two recent books, Standing and Van Parijs and Vanderborght restate the case for basic income on grounds that a regular income grant generates basic security,[34] and freedom to choose diverse life styles.[35] I argue that further underpinning the case for freedom and security with a case for human development and social equality is essential. Specifically, emphasizing developmental dimensions of freedom and equality shows how basic income is constitutively connected with democratization of the economy as a whole.[36] Basic income can be viewed in this context as a form of property in democratic society, using Macpherson's concept of democratic property as an 'individual property [that] extends to ... a right to a set of power relations that permits a full life of enjoyment and development of one's human capacities'.[37] It is as individuals depend on a civilization to flourish that we should think of the most basic resources within that civilization as subject to hybrid ownership arrangements: both individuals and society should have a share so that the stability and

15

commonality of the resource in question can be protected.[38]

To therefore defend basic income by emphasizing institutional aspects of democratic development, I build on the well-known human development approach associated with the Cambridge economist Amartya Sen. This school of thought is linked with two practical propositions I share: first, individuals' opportunities to flourish in society depend on public services playing an important role in the economy,[39] and second, when thinking about how public distribution and services should be devised, it is important to consider both human well-being and human powers to choose (capabilities).[40] So, for example, if someone needs additional resources to function, it is right that society should provide them, for example in the case of disability.[41] However, I add to this that we ought to regard the economy and human lives as involving developmental trajectories, which depend on existential stability in both the bodily and psychological senses. It follows that society should not just act to generate security in response to crises. In particular, to the extent that the global expansion of a new pervasive global competition economy has corroded public capacity to insulate human development, we need to extend the human development approach to affirm a more robust stance on governing the economy developmentally.

Accordingly, I add a new element to the established human development definition as the ability to function and choose.[42] Specifically, my definition of human development freedom also includes the power to have command of the process of one's life, one's doings and being over time, within society. Basic income can be considered necessary to secure this human development freedom because we live in societies where money governs access to a range of more specific choices, including to enter and leave employment and social relationships. Hence when individuals have to scramble for money, neither freedom nor civilization are possible.

Basic income changes the form in which security is given to a more independence-respecting kind for all. Doing so, basic income sets a challenge for us to rethink the form in which institutions and human activities are governed in general.

These considerations also provide an answer to another common concern related to the question of poverty: why give a regular income grant to those who already have money? The reasons present themselves when we stop thinking of basic income as just a means of consumption, and instead as an infrastructure of liberty and citizen equality.

17

Knowing one would receive this unconditional basic security – even during times when one does not need it urgently – can be considered a psychological and material shelter. The prevalence of knowledge that everyone else enjoys this security generates a framework of civic recognition of others, within which it is possible to conceive the breaking down of class barriers. Conversely, lack of an underlying structure of basic security is a trap for anyone in society who does not have enough money to secure a lifetime's subsistence. For example, an individual is stuck if she cannot imagine losing her job or leaving a household, or escape means-tested income support because taking a job would mean losing basic security. A person is also trapped if, when facing a crisis, he cannot access basic support in time, to support the life he has built, because all his savings must be exhausted first, as in the case of the means-tested benefit systems we have today. This raises the question: how did we get the welfare states we have?

Modern Civilization and Social Incorporation

Looking at basic income as simply necessary for reincorporation invites a re-examination of the elements of the modern civilization project. This project began with the birth of modern states in the sixteenth and seventeenth centuries, and from the outset was fraught with tensions and inconsistencies. The enlightenment idea of individual opportunity was contradicted by the modern process of unequal appropriation of resources (as Spence and Paine saw). Until the Second World War, income security systems emerged very slowly in the context of European states' jostle for power. When Titmuss wrote in 1965 of how in the postwar decades, 'social services on minimum standards for all citizens crept apologetically into existence', he captured the incremental as distinct from reasoned development of social assistance that had developed over several centuries.[43]

In conditions of postwar peace, welfare states became consolidated and expanded their remit and fiscal base. However, instead of taking the logical step of giving basic security to all, in capitalist democracies premised on property, new systems were set up in the form of insurance against market risk. The problem with this approach is that individuals do not control the labour market and may face many other risks.[44]

Despite these shortcomings, Titmuss, writing in the mid-1960s, reflected on how far Britain had travelled from the time of the Victorian Poor Laws. He appraised the movement that had occurred towards a protective state, away from the old punitive norms whereby 'Laws about poverty became associated with laws about crime', as there had been created 'a great many rules of expected behaviour, about work and non-work, property, savings, family relationships, co-habitation, men-in-the house [referring to laws requiring women to be genuinely single to receive support], and so forth'.[45] Looking back, Titmuss was satisfied to note how the old systems had been set aside as 'administratively grossly inefficient [given]; the discovery that … [with such systems the state] could not function effectively both as a redistributive agent and as an agent to prevent social breakdown'. Concluding his observations, he noted with confidence, 'All this is now … somewhat ancient history'. As it turned out, Titmuss's sense of relief was premature.

Cracks in the postwar edifice began to show not long after Titmuss's hopeful reflections. Postwar systems worked well in conditions of so-called 'embedded liberalism',[46] in which states planned occupations and the public sector, and supported business development, affordable housing, and systems of cooperation and settlement in labour relations. When these systems faced new pressures from the early 1970s onwards, and new structural forms of unemployment arose, rigid means-tested systems kicked in, and with added force allocated individuals to statuses outside the system, as unemployed, carer, ill, age-superfluous (as in early-retirement systems), and so on. It is no accident that the social scientist Esping-Andersen referred to modern welfare states – despite their varied form – as 'systems of stratification'.[47] The state actively generated the exclusions it then – through other policies – sought to treat.

The problems in postwar design gave ample cause to the ideational and political forces pushing states to retreat from their functions as entrepreneurial states. Raw capitalism re-emerged with vigour. The big forces pushing up inequality since then are well documented: until about 2000, wage compression and weakening of unions, and subsequently concentration of financial capital, monopolization linked with technology platforms, and political elitism.[48] The same forces that led to the rise in inequality altered the form and terms of social inclusion. It is this institutional trend which basic income contests. The 2008 financial crisis was the long-term fall-out of the abandonment of planned development in all its forms.

At stake is a new form of global governing and

adjusting through the labour market. The exclusionary effects of unplanned competition are diverse, ranging from the mass pool of graduates chasing fewer high-skill jobs,[49] to low-skill workers competing for unstable contracts.[50] Leading employers confirm zero-hours flexibility is a key way for private companies to manage global crises.[51] Along with a rise in involuntary part-time or fixed-time work,[52] trend-setting institutions, including large public and private service companies, have switched a growing slice of workers into non-standard employment, such as in Germany 'mini-jobs', or in the UK so-called 'zero-hours contracts'.[53,54] In the public sector, 'spot purchasing' practices linked with the drive to expand markets within the state are cited as the main reason behind the high concentration of zero-hours contracts in care services in the UK,[55] a trend also growing in Europe. The inability for workers on zero-hour contracts to plan family life, mortgages, and time for care is well documented:[56] the most vulnerable groups in society are today being cared for by the most vulnerable workers.

The job of basic income is not to endorse such developments but rather to help prevent their occurrence as a consequence of citizens' weak bargaining positions, individually and collectively. A relevant retort here would be to point out that stabilizing the funding and provision of public services, re-establishing occupational planning in education and in economic policy, and/or tightening labour laws, are the obvious solutions to the problems described: a basic income is not relevant here. But this is the wrong way of looking at it. Seeking to restabilize occupational life is a task of our time, but on a new basis: a return to the architecturally unstable reliance on employment as the sole mode of social incorporation would merely recreate the conditions for the crises of the 1960s and 1970s. The best institutions – the family, occupation, friendships and so on – are stronger when not all hangs on any one of them individually.

Hence, we can put the problem in another way: what *if* the right to basic income had been in place as a guarantee of individuals' autonomous existence. Would the trickle-down economics of stratified working and living have been able to fill the empty legal space created by the loopholes in postwar welfare design? Did the *absence* of a basic income generate the vacuum that made possible the encroachment on order in individuals' lives that we see today? Do we therefore *need* a basic income as a societal check on government, and a perpetual means of equality – an instrument to secure the democratic voice of citizens during the unfolding of their lives and in the evolution of the wider economy? If basic income did exist, other adjustment strategies, other public sector service delivery models, and more pressure by society on the state to support development planning to assist the choices of the young, may be more likely.

Unfreedom in Welfare – Crises of Incorporation

Notably, architects of the new market-led development model, like Milton Friedman, writing in the 1960s, argued for a version of basic income – the negative income tax (NIT), as a security net. Friedman foresaw the contradiction between his desire to make employment more flexible, and assistance systems built for stable employment. Thus, even if one may disagree with Friedman's wider notion of marketized development, one can see that his advocacy for the NIT was logically based. A NIT system would return at the end of the tax year the equivalent of the tax-free allowance to citizens whose earnings fell short. It was not exactly a rights-based system in the legal sense, but it aimed to guarantee some basic security. The system was never adopted.[57] Instead, states illogically adapted existing systems *to* the market, making access more difficult in order to push the project of full employment through making individuals take any available jobs, even as pay and conditions deteriorated.

The result is that modern states are undergoing a crisis in incorporation today, which stabs at the heart of the democratic project. The roll-out of sanctions policies – whereby benefit claimants become disentitled to benefits – has been stepped up since the 2008 financial crisis, together with public case-load reduction targets to support austerity goals across all mature economies. Contracting and sub-contracting out are involved, backed up by 'star ratings' systems to support case-load reduction.[58] In many countries, including the US, Italy and Ireland, a single refusal of a job offer can lead to permanent termination of support.[59] In the UK, a 2012 reform 'expanded the range of claimants subject to conditions and increased the maximum length of Jobseeker's Allowance sanctions from 26 to 156 weeks'.[60] In Denmark, Copenhagen municipality saw a more than four-fold increase in sanctioning between 2007 and 2010,[61] with 23.6% of all Danish claimants sanctioned that year, a similar level to in the UK.[62]

Sanctions have grown in an environment in which precaritization of working conditions is viewed positively as a source of absorbing the

2008 financial crisis: an OECD report a few years after the crisis argued that dismantling of collective representation and 'the regulation of working time' 'strengthened work incentives and increased the adaptability of firms', which helped 'better employment outcomes'.[63] Whilst there has been an increase in regulation to identify suitable wage levels and ethical concerns, meaning 'rights of claimants have ... been strengthened' in very specific instances,[64] the rise of systematic and intense checks on behaviour backed up by sanctions contradict the force of such exceptions. In 1980, less than 30% of OECD countries exercised consistent behavioural checks. By 2012, over 80% of countries did. In 1980, less than 20% of countries implemented sanctions. By 2012, nearly two-thirds did.[65] This represents an extraordinary if silent transition in the role of the state from notionally a bulwark against market encroachment to arbitrator of civic expulsion.

A result of the changes described is a new phenomenon of *social leakage*, defined as people that have fallen out of public records and formal society, as a result of policies that have discouraged the claiming of state benefits. Employability policies targeted at vulnerable groups backfire.[66] One study found that for every 100 sanctions applied in the UK, 22 persons exit from benefits without jobs.[67] This suggests the welfare regime contributes directly to informalizing society.[68]

As the UK National Audit Office puts it simply in a thorough report, sanctions that 'can be fixed in length up to three years', and can 'continue indefinitely', 'reduce support to people, sometimes leading to hardship, hunger and depression'.[69] Sanctions have been applied against failing to take jobs on irregular hours.[70] A rise in legal uncertainty about benefit status is cited as a key factor in a 134% rise in homelessness between 2009 and 2015 in the context of a growing private rental market in the UK,[71] with high benefit arrears a key factor in repossessions causing homelessness.[72] Figures collated in a government study reproduced on Calum's List suggest 4% of benefit disqualification or sanctions decisions are closely timed with people's deaths (81,140 cases of deaths), defined as 'date of death at the same time', between December 2011 and February 2014.[73]

Considering these conditions, a humanist case for basic income is a case against treating vulnerable states coercively, and against the distortion of public understanding of the civic foundation for human development that arises from this. Under a basic income, social work could be put to better use in solving the problem of 'how to reach the difficult to reach', as Titmuss highlighted in the 1960s as a neglected aspect of social policy.[74]

Pathways to Basic Income Reform

How remote is the scope for basic income reform? How is it linked up with broader changes? Offhand dismissal of basic income is often bound up with the wrong idea that basic income is all 'new' money. How much new money is involved depends on contexts and choices. In countries with more robust public finance, basic income involves primarily 'old' money: a switch in the form in which assistance is given. Basic income can be constructed from within tax and transfer systems without removing needs-based additional benefits, by reserving a share of such benefits unconditionally, and converting tax-free allowances.

Table 1 is a representation of what a very modest basic income – at the value of the lowest existing income benefit – would look like and cost in the UK. It is calculated by the UK Citizen's Basic Income Trust (CBIT), and is designed to hold everything bar the transition to a basic income constant. Based on the same conservative measure, table 2 shows how basic income would sit as a foundation under existing means-tested benefits, meaning that for those depending on them, a share would no longer be subject to means-test (or other conditions).

The CBIT's model is conservative in two senses. First, it assumes the existing low-wage, low-skill economy, which generates the need for in-work benefits to top up a basic income. Second, it accordingly assumes a tax model that exempts the lowest and highest earners. For example, the CBIT's calculation assumes the top tax category remaining at £150,000 on all levels of income above that figure.[75] In the CBIT calculations the cost of the transition falls on upper middle earners rather than decidedly the most wealthy in society. Notably, all states are advised by the IMF to look at raising the top levels of tax.[76] Despite its conservative traits, the CBIT scheme signals important positive impacts on reducing poverty and inequality. There is not a single way in which basic income can be financed or organized. Nor is it necessary to implement such a reform overnight. It is more important to consider the reasons the goal is valuable in the context of our time.

Table 1. An Illustrative Citizen's Basic Income Scheme

An evaluation of a Citizen's Basic Income (CBI) scheme with the working-age adult CBI set at £60 per week	
Citizen's pension per week (p.w.) existing state pension remains in place	£40
Working-age adult CBI p.w. (for individuals aged 25–64)	£63
Young adult CBI p.w. (for individuals aged 20–24)	£50
Education age CBI p.w. (16–19 year olds not in full-time education)	£40
Child Benefit is increased by £20 p.w.	(£20)
Income Tax rate increase required 3%	
Income Tax, basic rate (on £0–43,000)	23%
Income Tax higher rate (on £43–150,000)	43%
Income Tax, top rate (on £150,000+)	48%
Share of households in lowest income quintile suffering losses of over 10% at implementation	1.62%

		2.67%
Share of households in lowest income quintile experiencing losses of over 5% at implementation		
Share of all households experiencing losses of over 10% at implementation		1.9%
Share of all households experiencing losses of over 5% at implementation		9.88%
Net cost of scheme per annum		£2 billion

N.B. Figures are for the fiscal year 2017–18

Effects		Tax/benefits scheme 2017–18	Illustrative CBI scheme
Inequality	Disposable income Gini coefficient	0.30	0.27
Poverty*	Children	12%	8%
	Working-age adults in poverty	12%	9%
	Economically active working-age adults in poverty	4%	2%
	Elderly	11%	9%

Poverty is defined as the number in households with incomes below 60% of median equivalized household disposable income, and the Gini is calculated on a similar basis, based on Euro mod (Paola De Agostini, Euromod Country Report: https://www.euromod.ac.uk/ sites/default/files/country-reports/year8/Y8_CR_UK_Final.pdf, p. 70).

Source: Citizens' Basic Income Trust: *Citizen's Basic Income: A Brief Introduction*

Table 2. The Effect on Means-Tested Benefits

Fewer households would receive the main in-work and out-of-work means-tested benefits, and the value of claims would fall:

Table x Percentage of households claiming means-tested social security benefits for the existing and illustrative scheme in 2017	The existing scheme	The illustrative CBI
Percentage of households claiming benefits under …	12.7%	10.7%
Out-of-work benefits (income support, income-related Jobseekers' Allowance, income-related Employment Support Allowance)		
In-work benefits (Working Tax Credits and Child Tax Credits)	13.1%	10.8%
Pension Credit	6.2%	5.7%
Housing Benefit	16.2%	16.2%
Council Tax Benefit	21.0%	20.1%
Any means-tested benefits	33.2%	30.9%

32

Percentage reductions in total costs of means-tested benefits, and percentage reductions in average value of household claims, on implementation

	Reduction on total cost	Reduction in average value of claim
Out-of-work benefits	72.8	67.8%
In-work benefits	23.2	6.7%
Pension Credit	34.4	28.7%
Housing Benefit	3.2	2.9%
Council Tax Benefit	10.2	5.9%
All means-tested benefits	30.7	25.5%

Source: Citizens' Basic Income Trust, *Citizen's Basic Income: A Brief Introduction*

Basic Income and Development Goals

Why and how should we think about basic income in relation to wider social goals and economic reforms? An obvious reason for thinking through wider goals is that basic income embodies a humanist design of welfare and the economy: it is devised to support a person's independence and subsistence in a continuous and independence-respecting way. Hence, one needs to consider whether the background used as the basis for its defence is one that aligns or conflicts with this essential feature. Bringing the humanist – life-long and individual – form of basic income into view helps avert two forms of confusion.

The first is to do with the development model that grounds the basic income defence. Specifically, one should be careful not to take uncertainties linked with the globalization project as a necessary or positive background. Globalization cannot be the context against which a basic income is *justified*. A risk with rationalizing globalization is that basic income then becomes an anchor to justify norms and practices that are in direct conflict with the humanist and egalitarian values which the design of basic income embodies.

The way in which the humanist democratic

defence engages the form of institutions and governing of the economy directly marks it out from the libertarian case. Left libertarians are distinguished from right libertarians by wanting a higher level of basic income, if not initially, then eventually. On the other hand, right and left libertarian justifications for basic income share a tendency to take the global market model as, respectively, a fact or a good. Left libertarians have made the case for basic income as needed to replace the postwar order of 'stable positions', in which case we should accept that basic income is enough to generate stable positions, or stable (income and occupational) positions are a past value.[77] Left libertarians view a baseline of social welfare as necessary, though with clear limits.[78] On the other hand, right libertarians view socializing welfare as against inalienable rights of individuals to resources they can claim through the market.[79] This means left libertarians are equivocal about the use of the competition economy as a development model, whereas right libertarians see it as unequivocally good.

The classic left libertarian endorsement of basic income as a 'capitalist road to communism' suggested that basic income enables society to cross a bridge to a state in which paternalist authority is limited, leisure predominates, and the alienation connected with working for 'external rewards' ceases.[80] However, does this account situate the value and context of basic income in sufficiently broad terms? In seemingly endorsing self-determination in forging diverse life styles to a point that eviscerates collective governance, left libertarianism overdraws individuals' power in the global economy. The stress on direct transaction and choice makes social care rest too strongly on individual morals.

Van Parijs's four-pronged justice frame assumes the world is one we find and parcel out: resources are like a shipwreck, to be divided, jobs are naturally scarce, society is a 'massive gift distribution machine', and life is a time-profile.[81] The minimal job of states in this context is to ensure fair distribution of what exists to match the time-profile of people. On this basis, Van Parijs prioritizes basic income, alongside efficiency and individual responsibility. This then gives basic income a central and clear-cut market-justifying role. I defend basic income on different grounds, taking into account how economic development is dynamically rooted in institutions and plans humans create. Hence, prioritizing human development, it is the shape of institutions that ground human activities and social relations that should concern us collectively. In this case, the economics of human life is not about equal time-profiles, but about the equal value of developmental security. Basic income represents one dimension of development security necessarily bound to others.

More specifically, the democratic humanist case for basic income sees in basic income a mode of contesting competition as the primary social relation. Hence, in the democratic paradigm, committing to basic income should entail committing to humanist reform of the economy in other ways. Free exchange cannot be relied upon to generate human development-protective institutions directly. In this case, the competition economy is neither a fact nor an unalloyed good.

More specifically, the democratic case focuses on practical aspects of basic income – the thing basic income protects, i.e. life-long security. This means the mechanism – a simple equal payment (as a foundation within a wider set of protections) – is not a form of justice in itself, but a means to an end. Basic income is defended in terms of a human development ethics rather than a distributive ethics. This difference changes the character of other debates. To illustrate, it is common to set basic income next to proposals many view as in the same family on account of being distributive and targeting individuals. For example, to offer more ostensibly palatable versions or 'forerunners' or 'pathways' to basic income, a series of proposals for distributing capital grants to youth or working-age adults (a single grant of between £25,000 and £50,000) through citizens' wealth funds have re-emerged recently,[82] reviving an old debate about the choice between such grants and the life-long support a basic income presents.[83]

From a democratic development perspective, these two interventions are not directly comparable. First, basic income is distinctive because it is a continuing structure within the governing of the *whole economy*, whereas capital grants (CGs) leave the dynamic of the economy essentially intact. Second, basic income is a developmental structure for *individuals*, whereas CGs may or may not lead to a stable structure in a person's life. On their own, CGs reinforce the structure of personalized risk, and doing so they strengthen the values attending to punishing failure, and so potentially the justifiability of means-test and sanctions. On this basis, it is not clear that CGs are a good alternative to collective development policies, although they could be a component. In all, a focus on how the form of institutions and public policy generate complementarities in terms of human development invites an informationally broader view of cost and returns on investment.

Thinking of basic income as constitutive of human and economic development answers a number of more practical confusions, relating to the meaning of income and poverty, autonomy, and social equality and public reform, as I consider below.

Income and Poverty

The word 'income' makes people assume the intention with basic income is to put an end to employment or organized work, or that giving people 'free' money crowds out reasons to earn and contribute that are important. Basic income does the opposite, because it allows individuals to keep the grant when they earn. As such, basic income will take away the unfair disincentive of present income support systems that require persons to exhaust all their savings. If we think of secure subsistence as an infrastructure, like roads, or the Web, we can see how basic money can be considered enabling.

On the other hand, thinking of basic income as a *response* to poverty makes basic income a part of a compensatory rather than constitutive welfare paradigm, generating the problems listed earlier.[84] A case in point is the IMF's cautious case *for* basic income in states *without* adequate public administration,[85] and conversely a case *against* basic income in administratively developed societies.[86] It is hard not to see in this reasoning simply the restatement of deeply embedded bias: the old problem of 'unidentifiable causality' applied to public assistance. The idea that as mature welfare states have the apparatus to means-test, *therefore* targeting and careful administration of behaviour conditions are preferable, is like saying that no one should meet in person because we have Skype, or everything should be done via email, even when we know the phone is conflict-reducing because it is less formal. Like technology, administrative tools and systems have magnifying effects. The threat of having subsistence withdrawn is coercive, whether done by a computer or a public official. Some would say the former is worse. Modern societies generate technology so fast that mindless governing through the market can alter the function of institutions very quickly and imperceptibly. Modern society therefore requires more conscious awareness and debate of policies' constitutive norms, so that change can be filtered accordingly.

Autonomy and Human Development

Relatedly, emphasizing the rights and human development contribution of basic income also gives a wider frame to the argument for autonomy that is key in the case for basic income reform. The influential left libertarian advocate Philippe van Parijs reasoned that real choice between alternative life styles[87] would be optimized by favouring public distribution of money in equal shares.[88] Moreover, public funding should be prioritized to those things we actually use equally (preferably not, or less so, those we *might* need).[89] According to this paradigm, basic income stands, then, as an alternative – or at least is favoured – relative to a range of other institutional and regulatory approaches.[90] Therefore, the implication is that other modes of delivering welfare must defend themselves against this standard of strict egalitarian justice.

In contrast to this, a humanist perspective on democracy assumes that conditions for our freedom lie in society because in human life we depend on social conditions for our existence over time and in relation to others. Hence the concepts of autonomy and choice ought to be regarded as having a developmental and social component. Generating a foundation in which choices can have meaning in a social context and over time therefore warrants society to invest in and plan to support social opportunities through public provision and development regulation and planning.[91] Moreover, equality in justice requires public investment, an issue I take up in chapters 2 and 3. Accordingly, the democratic case, and the Foundation Model proposed here, entail a clear constraint on the level of the basic income against finance of other public services, justice systems and development investments.

Specifically, a democratic perspective on basic income does not see the distribution of basic income in a linear or zero-sum way. Rather, this approach entails defending two dimensions of universality at the same time: basic universality and universality of outcome. Basic universality (BU) encompasses those things we all need in *the same way* to function. Universality of outcomes (UO) are those things people require equal access to in different amounts to support human development outcomes, like good health, or active in an occupation. With respect to most human development goals, both BU and UO are involved in a good outcome. It makes very little sense to treat these issues as having equal cost: for example, the cost of roads or houses goes down when we share them, but this does not preclude us having individual incomes, and so on: sharing enables individual economy and vice versa.

Two key reasons libertarians in general prefer strictly equal sharing is that they worry about incorporating inequalities generated in the market into state provision, for example contributory pensions or other insurances that pay more to those able (through earnings) to put more in, or more to persons who choose to care or become unemployed. Second, they worry about paternalist arrangements that entail making decisions about welfare on people's behalf.[92]

In response to these worries, one can argue state schemes have many purposes. Sometimes alleviating insecurity – individually or collectively – requires unequal levels of support. Workers' mutual insurance against unemployment insures previous wages for a time to generate a soft-landing effect: even if you never use it, knowing it exists – for yourself or your children or spouse – is still a benefit. The human development defence of basic income operates on a principle of giving priority to developmental security. Hence, it does not require that all distributions should approach strict equality on principle. In fact, a basic income is not really strictly equal, since some people live longer. Ultimately, basic income *cannot* be defended on strict equality grounds.

On the second score, libertarians may be critical of needs-based welfare because it reduces persons' power to choose what welfare to have. However, this accent on actions as representations of liberty makes libertarians especially vulnerable to not recognizing the importance and role of public empathy in protecting liberty. This is easier to understand when we think of a person who cannot act to claim liberty, or who may not be able to command empathy through social relations, which is any group that suffers physical, mental, or social impairments. By definition, persons in vulnerable positions cannot self-organize, hence self-organization as a route to welfare protects the strong. Specifically, rationing health for older people to raise average consumption conflicts with humanist norms. It also conflicts with the principle of life-long income security on grounds of freedom: knowing health care or security diminishes as we get older would cut down the security experienced when we are young.

Hence, just as basic income is important as a foundation, it cannot be the whole structure in terms of the allocation of monetary and other resources. The basic premise of this argument is that individuals cannot generate and anticipate all the services they need, and the burden of self-organization is also a form of unfreedom. A relational welfare model assumes that society and individuals function better where basic security is paralleled with stable opportunities and social outreach to foster many points of inclusion in society.

So why is it important to defend strict equality at all? In response, some strict equality is important to defend income entitlements on a rights basis and to secure a permanent state and sense of autonomy. The strictly equal form of the basic income mimics as best it can a condition of guaranteed access which is essential in basic goods. It is architectural in the sense that it generates a foundation for humanist policies. In the case of political participation, a foundation is the principle of one person, one vote. On top of this, persons may choose to join political parties or stand for office, write political columns in newspapers, or join other civic organizations. Assuming a basic income similarly can be combined with other ways of distributing income streams and shares is hardly radical, but simply elementary.

Social Equality and Public Reform

Emphasizing the importance of a humanist form of core institutions, a democratic case for basic income also sets out a different course to piecemeal public reform of income assistance.

Policy innovations since the 1990s have focused on market-readiness, not individuals' security and freedom to plan working life or choose employment. In systems that still condition support on taking available jobs, Working Tax Credits are a subsidy of low-paid jobs, giving individuals little choice. The tapering away of assistance with earnings can act to destroy incentives to earn in what are often considered unattractive (unchosen) jobs. In-work conditionalities entail that persons can be asked to change jobs they like if another job has more hours.[93] Moreover, means-tests are generally set up so that that in order to receive public support, you must own nothing, or not very much. A consequence of this is to put the status of owning and saving into doubt, generating ownership traps that are both a disincentive to effort and a source of injustice in public policy.

Consequently, the Foundation Model put forward here entails an architectural vision of economic security, in which basic income aids in the construction and maintenance of membership of other key democratically constituted institutions in society. From this perspective, basic income is viewed as a small but significant part in the way systems work:

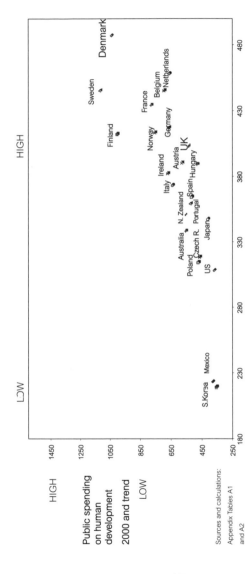

Sources and calculations:
Appendix Tables A1
and A2

Public revenue: Index of 1. Total tax revenue in GDP 2000 and trend 1975-2000, 2. Top marginal tax rate and multiple at which it sets in, 2000, and trend. 3. Levels of corporate income tax on distributed profits, 2000. 4. Net statutory tax rates on dividend income (shareholder level), 2000. 5. Overall personal income tax and corporate income tax rates on dividend income, 2000. 6 Statutory corporate income tax rate, 2000. 7. Corporate tax revenue as % of GDP; 2000 and trend 1982-2000.

Public spending on human development: Index o ' 1. Public expenditure in GDP 2000, and trend, 2000-15. 2. Public social expenditure in GDP; 2000, and trend, 1990-2014. 3. Public expenditure on education in GDP 1995, and trend, 1995/6-2006. 4. Public expenditure on education in social expenditure. 2000, and trend 1998-2005. 5. Public spending on training, job creation and supported employment 2000 and trend 1995-2006. 6. Public spending on child-care in GDP; 1998, and trend 1998-2005.

Figure 1. Public Revenue and Public Spending on Human Development, 2000 and Trend

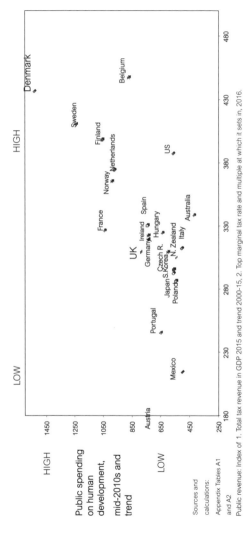

Public revenue: Index of 1. Total tax revenue in GDP 2015 and trend 2000-15, 2. Top marginal tax rate and multiple at which it sets in, 2016.
3. Levels of corporate income tax on distributed profits, 2009. 4. Net statutory tax rates on dividend income (shareholder level), 2009.
5. Overall personal income tax and corporate income tax rates on dividend income, 2009. 6 Statutory corporate income tax rate, 2009.
7. Corporate tax revenue as % of GDP. 2016 and trend 2000-16.
Public spending on human development: Index of 1. Public expenditure in GDP 2015, and trend 2000-15. 2. Public social expenditure in GDP,
2014, and trend. 1990-2014. 3. Public expenditure on education in GDP, 2011, and trend, 1995-2011. 4. Public expenditure on education in
public expenditure, 2011, and trend, 1995-2011. 5. Public spending on training, job creation and supported employment 2013, and trend,
2006-13. 6. Public spending on child-care in GDP, 2011, and trend, 2005-11.

Figure 2. Public Revenue and Public Spending on Human Development, mid-2010s and Trend

48

basic income is both instrumental to a wider governance change, and to some extent dependent on that change. It can be expected that basic income will not enjoy stability without a wider democratic setting.

To illustrate, in Nordic states with less wage corrosion and higher labour standards, transfers have remained primarily welfare-orientated, whereas in Anglo-liberal states a growing trend is towards wages subsidy.[94] Exemplifying the built-up governance capabilities at stake, figures 1 and 2 compare developed countries in terms of their support of human development, and the link with universality in other policies and systems of tax. The index of public spending on human development includes general public, social, education, training, and childcare expenditure in GDP, as well as trends over time. The public revenue score includes the level and trend in tax revenue as a percentage of GDP, levels and trends in dividend income and corporate taxation, as well as the distribution of tax across income groups. Rather than take just one measure, such as taxation in GDP, the index gives a more robust picture of how inclusive tax contribution is, which tends to be a proxy for other things, such as how dispersed wage-setting is. Consider that tax systems that exempt large sectors of low-wage work actually help sustain low-wage employment. On this score, systems where the highest rate of tax sets in at high multiples of the average wage are more redistributive but less cooperative and typically linked with a smaller public share of the whole economy, as both average and top rates of tax tend to be lower. Larger fiscal publics also tend to publicly own and/or regulate resource use to a larger extent, reinforcing capacity to support human security. More 'cooperative' systems, typically social democratic states, usually have lower wage dispersions, and relatively less precarious labour markets. In these states, public finance of a set of complementary human development services is possible and more likely, as figures 1 and 2 show, which supports incorporation, reinforcing the system.

In all, the democratic human development case for basic income has four distinctive features. First, it is architectural: basic income is a foundation within a necessarily more complex economic security structure, emphasizing public support and sources of contribution. Second, it is progressive: the institutional change a basic income heralds is more important than the initial level of basic income; regard for other institutions and their finance means a realistic transition builds gradually within the cooperative structures of different societies. Third, a democratic humanist case is governance-focused: it is assumed the institutional support of human development is systemic, emphasizing the role of the state and strategic planning. Fourth, the case made is constitutive of human development freedom: it is assumed freedom is constructed through stable institutions in society.

To summarize, a general problem with modern social protection systems is that they are conceived as security *against risk*. Like the story of the keyboard that was badly designed when invented in the nineteenth century, but then got 'stuck' as more and more manufacturers used it,[95] the notion of means-tested basic assistance is a case of lock-in of an essentially degrading form of social relation. It is important to be secure against risk. However, this should be the function of additional (voluntary or contributory) social insurance arrangements. We insure our house against risk on the assumption the house itself is secured in some other way (we lock it; we are not ourselves going to start a fire). We insure our life against accident or death on the assumption of a shared health service and a commitment to lead – on the whole – healthy lives. Similarly, from backward-looking risk to forward-looking incentives to plan, save and share risk, basic income transforms the architecture of governance.

The fact that basic income does not exist, or may be slow to come into being, if we took a step in that direction now, is not an argument against basic income as such. We do not now look back at the introduction of universal suffrage and think it was not worth having because it took over 150 years to come into being – as in the case of Britain, from the Ballot Act of 1872, which introduced secret voting, to full franchise of men and women in 1928. The fact that basic income is supported by what many regard as populist movements and political parties also is no ground to dismiss it: supporters of universal suffrage were viewed as populists or troublemakers in their day.

What is needed is to turn from a view of basic income as protest or utopian fantasy to a broader account of basic income against principles we can recognize in the wider debate about freedom in economy, welfare and society. Accordingly, in the next chapter I discuss in more detail how basic income can be seen as constitutive of human development and humanist governance and norms.

2

Human Development Freedom

The way that basic income is organized to provide security unconditionally over a whole lifetime gives humanist principles priority over the market. Indicating what is at stake in such a shift, in the last chapter, I suggested that society has to be constructed and that basic income is important in that continuing task. In this chapter, I assess in more detail the standards against which a basic income's constructive role may be thought about. Accordingly, I first briefly draw out how market justice has redefined social policy as at once anti-poverty policy, and a foundation for financialized markets. I then consider how defending basic income as a contrasting form of humanist governing extends on the influential human development approach. Next, I give evidence and practical reasons to think a basic income supports humanist

53

standards and norms in society, and in doing so supports systems of justice and justice prevailing.

Social Policy and Market Justice

Considering basic income as a life-long structure invokes humanist norms that once were central to policy discourse. For postwar reformers, the human life cycle provided the background for conceptions of freedom. Writing in 1949, T.H. Marshall lamented how, 'A man of 40 may be judged by his performance in an examination taken at the age of 15. The ticket obtained on leaving school or college is for a life journey.'[1] Relatedly, when the psychologist Erich Fromm, who supported basic income on humanist grounds,[2] wrote in the 1960s about a 'longing for complete laziness', he referred to the effect of demeaning work, when a person has 'no part in planning the work process, no part in its outcome'.[3]

Come the 1970s, social policy turned the clock back to emphasize the moral correction of the poor, but this time through refined use of market ideology and economic science, resurrecting on a new principled basis the competitive standardization Marshall had worried about. The theory of market equilibrium in economics extended to social policy through applying the idea of a leisure–work trade-off to the management of income security.[4] According to this law – under any circumstances – we hate to work, and always prefer leisure. In both developing and developed countries, this thinking has underpinned anti-poverty policies constructed to retain fear of subsistence insecurity as a mechanism to motivate work: in developing countries setting grants so low that in many cases nutritional objectives could not be met.[5]

In terms of justification, the marketization project has generally been characterized by vague reference to necessity,[6] and some sweeping arguments. For example, when in the early 1980s, Hayek cast labour unions as the sources of market failure,[7] he let corporate conglomerates off the hook. Even so, this early stage of the market project involved a fairly clear discourse about abating monopoly, and – crucially – underpinning new private service models with a baseline of less discriminating public provision. To illustrate this, the path-breaking work of Mead and his colleagues, published in 1997 to defend the new moralism in the US context, is very instructive.[8] Framed against an attack on the 'structuralist thesis', Mead et al. drew up welfare reform goals around public case-load reduction in favour of private provision.[9] In the case of the homeless, using private provision would reinforce individual responsibility (attacking the 'disordered life of the homeless') through the threat of sanction (eviction).[10] Welfare policies should address the 'immediate' (personal) rather than underlying 'ultimate' (social) causes of poverty.[11]

Notably, however, despite the strong emphasis on privatization and moralism, proponents of the new agenda at this stage acknowledged that the sanctions regime operating in private shelters relied on a baseline of free public provision: 'Because clients have no right to a particular shelter, private shelters may require and enforce participation in their program *as long as* noncompliant clients are free to return to a general shelter' (emphasis added).[12] 'It is because clients make a *voluntary choice* to go to a certain program shelter that the shelters can reasonably expect clients to adhere to their programs.'[13] In this context, it is also recognized that sanctions are not intended to be enforced; 'the contracts are primarily a management tool rather than sources of realistic sanctions'. 'A client's problems are recognized and resolved by worker and resident working together in an individualized relationship of *mutual respect* and *reciprocal accountability*' (all emphases added).[14] We can glean from the above how supporters of privatization in the 1990s thought this line of reform relied on an *unconditional tier*, which is analogous to the thinking behind the institutional case for basic income as a foundation for other social systems and social justice itself. The unacknowledged corrosion of public and humanist standards and principles that has occurred since begs therefore a return to first principles: what informs humanist standards and norms and their legal support?

Before considering wider reasons, we can begin by noting how basic income is an institution which expresses humanist norms. However justified, giving persons life-long, regular, basic income is humanist in the sense that it is a developmental provision, designed to support agency and self throughout a whole life. Notably, libertarian basic income supporters also claim basic income is important because it supports individuals' power to choose in a continual form, and in this sense adhere to a (delimited) form of humanist commitment.[15] On the other hand, as argued in chapter 1, humanism may still be at risk if basic income is understood in terms of an otherwise minimal welfare state. As an example, World Bank advocates of market equilibrium economics have turned recently to argue for a 'revenue neutral switch from existing welfare programs to a basic income' of a global 'basic income capitalism' variety.[16] In this case, offering basic income as a poverty remedy in the context of the global 'race to the bottom'[17] places basic income strategically as a compensatory redistributive policy in a context of low-skill, fragmented employment, and debt-finance of welfare and services.[18] The humanism within basic income is put to the service of an economic agenda that is not humanist in orientation or application.

Human Development and Humanist Justice

Addressing the above problems, I want to explore how an institutional perspective, backed up by research on human motivation and health, supplements the well-known human development approach (HDA), in such a way that basic income can be defended within this paradigm. Accordingly, in this chapter, I consider further what a democratic humanist perspective entails both in relation to the human development approach and for rethinking the competition economy. Specifically, whereas the HDA has maintained a position of neutrality on the design of institutions in order to protect open-ended choice,[19] an institutional perspective entails thinking through what the forces are that generate and shape institutions in society.

On that basis, what does a humanist perspective entail, more specifically? First, a humanist perspective on governing might recognize how modalities of human life itself – developmental processes like learning, working and caring, and social relations these activities involve – give rise to institutions that shape the opportunities we have. These are listed as 'developmental institutions' in figure 3. From this we can generate two theses, about freedom, and about the necessity of cooperation for freedom. First, human development freedom is a valuable state that involves attaining forms of overall command of developmental processes that shape individuals' lives. This can be envisaged as enjoying different forms of control of human time (developmental freedoms) and social relations (relational and cooperative freedoms, figure 3). However, second, this entails a strong collective action problem because of how we inescapably form part of settings like the family, education and workplaces (developmental institutions) that deeply affect us, yet we cannot control. In short, our freedom is always constrained by institutions, and because this is the case, we all have interests in a humanist design and form of governing of at least the institutions we most need.

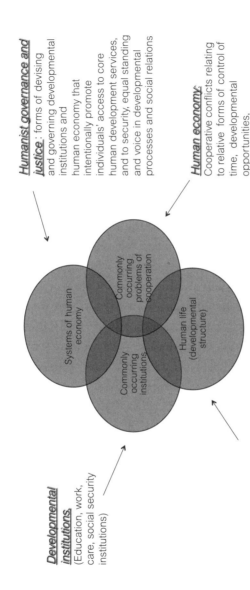

Humanist governance and justice: forms of devising and governing developmental institutions and human economy that intentionally promote individuals' access to core human development services, and to security, equal standing and voice in developmental processes and social relations

Human economy: Cooperative conflicts relating to relative forms of control of time, developmental opportunities, social and personal security and voice in social relations

Developmental institutions: (Education, work, care, social security institutions)

Human ecology: Modalities of human development linked with existential needs, cognitive powers, social dependence and interests in overall self-development, and command of time and leisure

Labels within diagram:
- Systems of human economy
- Commonly occurring problems of cooperation
- Commonly occurring institutions
- Human life (developmental structure)

Figure 3. Human Economy

In this context, human development justice can be defined by universality of *access* to core human development resources and services governing incorporation and equality in society. For example, this would make a case for an unconditional tier of access to housing and income, as already exists in schooling and health in most countries.

Humanist justice in governing, on the other hand, can be defined by the *form of rules* that frame the delivery of said services and the governance of other key institutions and services. In general, we can assume that when the rules ensure permanence of essential resources, as in the case of basic income and life-long health insurance, this generates a valuable, constant sense of control in different settings (figure 4).

In all, we can surmise humanist governance is important because it affects the circumstances we receive: how far we need to bargain and strive to get good conditions, or we are free to inherit and enjoy them. But what is, and what informs, humanist governance, more specifically? In answer to this, setting forth humanist standards for institutions entails going further in terms of specification of norms and policy actions than is standard in the human development approach. For example, the human development scholar Martha Nussbaum is

A state of enjoying developmental freedoms: control of time, activities and social relations

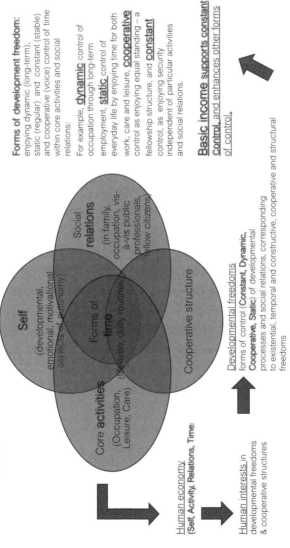

Self
(developmental, emotional, motivational aspects of autonomy)

Social relations
(in family, occupation, vis-à-vis public professionals, fellow citizens)

Forms of time
(lifetime, daily routines)

Core activities
(Occupation, Leisure, Care)

Cooperative structure

Forms of development freedom:
enjoying dynamic (long-term), static (regular) and constant (stable) and cooperative (voice) control of time within core activities and social relations:

For example, **dynamic** control of occupation through long-term employment, **static** control of everyday life by enjoying time for both work, care and leisure, **cooperative** control as enjoying equal standing – a fellowship structure, and **constant** control, as enjoying security independent of particular activities and social relations.

Basic income supports constant control, and enhances other forms of control.

Human economy
(Self, Activity, Relations, Time)

Human interests in developmental freedoms & cooperative structures

Developmental freedoms
forms of control (**Constant, Dynamic, Cooperative, Static**) of developmental processes and social relations, corresponding to existential, temporal and constructive, cooperative and structural freedoms

Figure 4. Human Development Freedom

generally known to be more interested than other theorists such as Sen in drawing up a generic *list* of human capabilities – things all humans would choose – like playing, or feeling secure.[20] On the other hand, like libertarian arguments for basic income, Nussbaum has emphasized public minima, rather than broader systemic conditions for human development.[21] This means we cannot be sure either approach would necessarily want to defend basic income as an element in humanist governing – as an independent regulatory provision, and by extension other such provisions. For example, Nussbaum is equivocal about how much public intervention is acceptable to promote girls' equal education and occupation opportunities in the context of communal rights to protect traditional care roles.[22]

This seems to leave a vacuum in terms of a clear defence of developmental rights and integrity. The implication is that we cannot judge what are standards of human development protection, including how the competition economy ought to be limited.

Accordingly, the institutional approach I set out builds on, yet goes beyond, the HDA in three ways, related with recognizing constraints on *choice*, *institutions' form*, and freedom in *modernity*. First, regarding *choice*, we can think of freedom in terms of – as Sen suggests – a 'constitutive plurality' in which different freedoms have independent importance.[23] Yet, we can also consider how the experience of human development freedom entails not having to trade one form of freedom for another. So, for example, we may have a stable job but no real opportunity to leave, because we lack constant control ('free' basic income or health care). We may lack control of our daily schedule (static control) if workloads are intense or erratic, or there is not sufficient child-care. Finally, we may not enjoy cooperative control, if in education or work there is constant competition with peers, or in the family our welfare comes second to that of others. In any or all of these cases, having a stable job or family life (enjoying dynamic control and social security) is no longer as supportive of our well-being as may be presumed from the outside (figure 3).

In turn, this highlights the reasons for wanting to capture more precisely the coercive effects of competition processes, and hence the need and ways to limit their extent both in production processes and in public services. The way in which Marshall saw the social rights developed after the Second World War as necessary to give substance to formal opportunities linked with the market springs to mind. An example of merely civil rights he gave was having free speech with inferior education, which meant that you may have a right to speak, yet 'have nothing to say that is worth saying, and no means of making yourself heard if you say it.'[24]

In all, the systemic context in which human activities are shaped forces us to think again about the design of core institutions in terms of implications for humanist justice. For example, it is not satisfying to think of what the human development theorist Robeyns calls 'tragic' choices – between working ('providing for my family') and 'properly car[ing] for and supervis[ing] my children'[25] – as choices individuals reasonably can or ought to have to make.[26] Rather, choice sets that (tragically) trade off core human activities (a species of what the HDA terms 'functionings') can be viewed as *structures of choices* that individuals should not be subjected to (under just institutions). This is, then, a reason we should set the case for basic income together with a case for other rights constitutive of human development freedom, such as rights to real opportunities for occupation, welfare and care – as well as rights to a life free from debt and social exclusion. Involved is a rethink of the institutional foundations we have inherited.

To illustrate the issues at stake, we can take note of how theorists of comparative capitalism have identified a historical link between the formation of competition and coercion. For instance, scholars have linked early repressive forms of capitalism with casualization.[27] In the Anglo-liberal context, traditions of managerial control in work followed.[28] When postwar Keynesianism waned in the 1970s, the underlying conditions existed which precipitated the shift towards greater reliance on punishment in social policy (figure 5).[29]

In this wider context, the case for basic income can be linked with a normative and institutional shift in governing today.[30] Specifically, we can assume that the existence of independent security is important in shaping relations of work, as well as service providers' relation with citizens. In the case of labour relations, the postwar welfare and legal framing of employment, which washed out the repressive roots of capitalist development to some extent, gave workers a degree of control. For example, sanctions policies in top-up contributory systems of income support were linked with initial waiting periods to ward off incentives to 'job-hop'. A system driven in that way by *ex-ante* incentives left individuals with a reasonable measure of control and choice, whilst containing cost. To the extent the multi-layered systems of security have disappeared, today individuals are left more vulnerable. With regard to services, a relevant hypothesis in this context is that the work

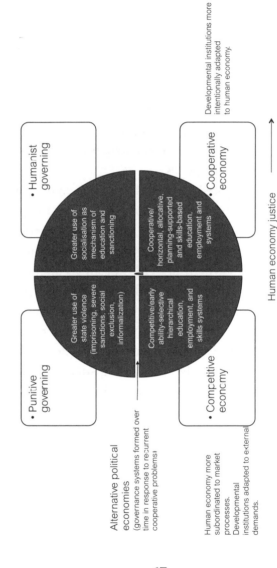

Figure 5. Political Economies of Punitive and Humanist Governing

• Punitive governing

• Humanist governing

Greater use of state violence (imprisoning, severe sanctions, social exclusion, informalization)

Greater use of socialisation as mechanism of education and sanctioning

Competitive/early ability-selective hierarchical education, employment, and skills systems

Cooperative/horizontal, allocative, planning-supported and skills-based education, employment and systems

• Competitive economy

• Cooperative economy

Human economy justice

Alternative political economies
(governance systems formed over time in response to recurrent cooperative problems)

Human economy more subordinated to market processes.
Developmental institutions adapted to external demands.

Developmental institutions more intentionally adapted to human economy.

of public professionals – social workers, teachers, judges, doctors – becomes more difficult to perform in the absence of basic security in society, because then power inequalities and status uncertainties intercede in their work. To illustrate further, next I discuss how hard facts of human ecology – existential need, constructive cognitive powers, social dependence, and reliance on structure – make the case for stable structures.

As already noted, whereas the HDA has looked at human function in terms of activities in the present (eating, playing, being secure) and the role of choice (eating versus fasting), we can also consider the patterns in which activities occur as shaped by core human constraints and propensities (*human ecology*, figure 3). An important aspect of these hard human facts is that developmental processes like learning and caring occur in a sequence, over time. They also involve continuing social relations. Accordingly, to break down why basic income is important on grounds of human security and can be justified in terms that also make a case for other stable structures, in the next sections I look at the case for humanist governance in relation to the above-listed developmental underpinnings of human functioning. These are existential need, cognition, dependence and reliance on structure.

Existential Need and Security

Security to support existence is a shared human need. Against this, a positive case can be made for basic income as part of an essential security structure to support human functioning, as well as avert injustice and tragedy. With regard to the positive case, there is a body of evidence that security in the near environment is a condition of health and human functioning. Experimental research has shown that problem-solving ('slow thinking') is linked with the absence of pressure – the opportunity to 'stop'.[31] Findings that residents in cities that paid cash grants over a longer period found this 'normal',[32] young people stayed longer in school, and mental health improved,[33] tally with knowledge we have that external security leads persons to utilize their time more rationally,[34] and stable cash grants reduce worry.[35]

Other research has shown social dysfunction and ill-being arise from senses of loss of personal control over daily life.[36] Uncontrollable events induce helplessness.[37] Against this evidence, a basic income can be considered simply elementary to insure against human breakdown in a modern economy governed by money. An assurance of basic subsistence might forestall cases of individuals taking their own lives over petty debts.[38] It might help prevent tragic outcomes linked with benefit disqualification or sanctions, discussed in the previous chapter. A system of proving ill health to achieve basic security is paradoxical considering insecurity is a known cause of ill health.[39] Against this, basic income can be considered an institution of health, as well as contributory to public systems of health. Health services that become involved in administering social security are compromised. A separate guarantee of subsistence may pre-empt the case where doctors face difficult decisions concerning medical certificates needed to extend persons' right to income security. The British TV personality and general practitioner (GP) Ranjan Chatterjee, in reacting to the idea of basic income, referred to the often banal reasons for benefit sanctions, and patients approaching their GP to have sick-notes backdated to retain subsistence, as the 'system everyone has to play to get an outcome'.[40]

The competition economy disrupts human schedules at all levels of society. According to a leading commercial healthcare sector lawyer, zero-hours economies create low morale and a system in which it becomes in employers' interests for staff to not perform well: 'One of the biggest risks of using a temporary worker is that the person turns out to be a good performer who is then offered shifts on a regular basis, which in turn increases the likelihood that they will be regarded by an employment tribunal as an employee with full employment rights.'[41] However, a rise in perverse incentives within the management of staff performance is not confined to zero-hours contracts. The breaking-up of work into smaller and smaller accounting management units is a reality in more stable occupations as well, making attempts to raise the long-term effectiveness of work and learning an offence against the system. Hence, the language of workfare, which problematizes the question whether people want to work, skirts over a deeper problem, which is whether they can, given a growing difficulty in actually being productive, in both formal work and care, within a unit-managed economy. In this sense, the behaviour accounting system involved in income assistance access is a window into the wider society. For example, a theme that recurs on blog sites about the effect of complicated systems of access to basic security is the way burden-of-proof systems and long waiting periods undermine persons' status and ability to command authority in social roles, like parenting. As one woman put it, referring to Britain's Universal Credit (UC), which has been accused of using long waiting periods and bureaucratic procedures to deter claims,[42] 'I think that the UC – the way it works is a breach of children's rights. It puts children at a risk of neglect by their own parents and in their own families. It forces the parents to show the children that being in arrears, entering payment agreements, facing eviction is a way of living.'[43]

The case of individuals who feel coerced by society in ways that destroy their opportunities to carry out basic duties with dignity in work or care illustrates how all kinds of social relations that construct society are at stake in the case of guaranteeing the human right to subsistence. A basic income does not by itself generate more stable work schedules, but it allows the question to be posed. In so far as then basic income represents mental assurance, it acts like a vaccine does, to support the natural immune system, rather than – as unstable support does – breaking it down. In protecting the status of individuals in the economy, basic income protects justice and coherence in public spending. Starting from the bottom of society, it helps roll back injustice and connect up efforts made in social policy to reduce deprivation, considering how new poverty and new injustice are created when sanctioning a parent involves being blind to the child.

Cognitive Development and Stability

A basic income recognizes a form of status independence that is important for human function. Removing arbitration in determining individuals' right to existence supports an inclination to think long-term that is natural to humans: having to negotiate a situation as dire as simply survival disrupts this natural intention. There is a solid body of literature that points to an innate human orientation to learn, create and exchange learning through *time*.[44] The economist Douglas North[45] relied on evidence that human learning is sequence-based to argue that humans thrive in conditions of calculated risk where strategizing is backed up by certainty. Basic income mimics in individuals' lives the role limited liability law is designed to play to encourage business confidence through the severance of subsistence from enterprise failure. Studies comparing income support systems have shown that provisions that give persons more generous income security outside the labour market *for longer* tend to lead to longer employment.[46] We also know that individuals are generally motivated by occupational values, and are more likely to enjoy work for itself when they have several independent sources of economic security.[47]

Relatedly, neuroscience research has linked health outcomes with the opportunity for eudemonic well-being, associated with longer-term and noble goals beyond immediate self-gratification.[48] In the same context, overall greater well-being has been connected with the ability to integrate daily tasks with life-long goals.[49] Earning and learning to enjoy a skill involves thousands of hours of practice over a long period of time, as well as a community of learning, presupposing, therefore, the existence of stable schedules and occupational institutions.[50] In modern states, schooling is compulsory. But at school, practices to teach children by ability at the earliest age are becoming more common as a consequence of the competition framework within public education. To aid schools in 'proving' performance, children can be placed in sets where from the start they aspire to a medium-range or lower grade. Arguing for basic income as a right to human development intercedes here in the sense that it begs a consideration of the value of sheltering processes of learning, and fellowship in learning, working, and care. A humanist case for basic income is also a case for a form of learning and working without constant competition and testing.

Human Development Freedom

Dependence and Fellowship

Relatedly, there is reason to assume basic individual security is essential to construct cooperation in care and within affective relations, across gender and in society. Cooperation in care and other activities is linked with mental and physical health.[51] Our need for care – and caring unions in family life – can be considered the hardest of the human facts, a need that cannot be manipulated or changed. In this context, individual insecurity extends the forces that support inequality in gender and other affective relations. A recent, for example, study suggests that economic insecurity linked with gender inequality generates conditions for civil war.[52] Similarly, to describe the problem of cooperation, the economist Hirschman stressed the importance of exit *and* voice in social relations. The role of basic income in relation to exit has been discussed. Exit backs up the power to say no: to leave or refuse.[53] Here instead I emphasize how basic income backs up the power to have voice within relations we cannot or do not want to leave. Individual security supports equality within a system of developmental institutions within society.

To see more clearly how basic income supports more equal affective relations in society and cooperation in care we need to explain how coercion can build up in social relations when individuals do not enjoy independent security. Dependent relations – defined as any we are bound to by affection, duty or complex ties, such as to a difficult boss in a job we like – are different from casual acquaintances. An acquaintance can be dropped if we find the exchange is unequal. Not so with dependent ties. In this case, a *succession* of unequal exchanges can produce gradually a power imbalance that is hard to reverse. To further illustrate, whereas cumulative inequality is a problem we recognize in labour relations and capitalism as a whole, in the private domain, such as relations in the family, inequality inequality may be less visible. Here, Sen's illuminating analysis of cooperative conflict in the family is relevant to an understanding of the problem of care relations within the wider economy. Sen argues that women's subordination (in the family) occurs as an outcome of a succession of conflicts.[54] However, where Sen associates women's vulnerability occasioned by childbirth with primitive social life,[55] we might also consider the affective obligation that begins in a pregnancy and in childbirth as a status and bond that has a structure that positions in most cases – if not only – mothers in a different relation to others from that point on. Modernity has not changed this fact. Further supporting the contention that choice in modernity does not necessarily support gender equality, research on urban labour markets has shown that individuals across different social strata value occupational goals, yet women face greater care–occupation trade-offs.[56] Consequently, in a competition framework, especially, there is a risk of power imbalance building *in and across* settings, like work and the home. In turn, this puts especially women at risk of being in a double fix: a state of being progressively undermined.

Irregularity in income and work schedules exacerbate these inequalities, which have been shown to be cross-cutting but greater for the lowest earners.[57] So it is a deep consideration of justice whether or not public systems enable this kind of state to occur. In the absence of stable individual structures, including effective subsistence guarantees, but also developmental regulations to lower workloads, and promote equal care, we can say governance is human economy unjust. In such conditions, women as mothers are (especially) likely to face a double tragedy: on the one hand, there is the tragic choice of caring or working, and the further corollary that making the choice entails abandoning overall freedom. On the other hand, a woman who still tries to attain that overall freedom will be faced with being outperformed in both work and care. A life is merely a life of never making it.

State action can improve or make matters worse, in ways that implicate justice in how access to income security is governed. Research on cash grants has shown families in receipt of time-delimited grants are often worse off in socio-psychological terms than before support began.[58] Support that narrows or ends unforeseeably puts individuals metaphorically speaking in the position of cyclists navigating cycle lanes that end just as the road narrows, compromising safety without warning. In Europe today, the most important sources of self-reported low well-being relate to insecurity in income and housing.[59] Lack of entitlement to settlement in society may be the most urgent injustice of our day, not only as it promotes exclusion, but because of the way it leads individuals semi-unconsciously into criminality.

A relevant example is young single mothers falling foul of rules which condition their subsistence and housing security on boyfriends not staying overnight. A public defence lawyer dealing with such cases put part of the problem down to absent fathers. In these cases, the women were triply vulnerable, left to undertake responsibilities for children, unsure of their relationship and income status, and – unwittingly – gaining a criminal record.[60] Involved in these contemporary cases is a return of the 'man in the house' rules that Titmuss – writing in 1965 and quoted in chapter 1 – thought 'discriminatory' and 'ancient history'.

Notably, if we focused narrowly on – say – universality in rule application, we might not be able to pinpoint what went wrong in these cases where young mothers were criminalized. If, however, we apply humanist principles to the problem, we can.

Basic income also intervenes in the modern competition and choice framework in a more general way. Basic income contributes to ensure care relations and vulnerabilities do not become conditions for social coercion. At stake here is not (as some have emphasized) the right of women (or men) to choose work *or* care (even if this is also relevant). A preceding and more wide-ranging role of basic income is to help reduce the competitive pressures that put all individuals in a position to make those choices.

The Unitary Self and Control over Time

Finally, the case of care relations bears out the earlier more general contention made that overall control of time is essential for freedom. Although an immediate connection can and has been made between basic income and control of work and leisure,[61] and between leisure and freedom,[62] we have to be careful in simply assuming that having access to leisure can do the work.

Comparison of mature economies suggests that greater overall control of time in different settings coincides with more cooperative economies. To exemplify this, figure 6 gives a measure of how much control people have in work, and how much control they have over time overall in different societies. The data on control in work is a composite measure of how much control people feel they have over tasks and time at work, and well-being at work. In addition, it measures how equal the scores are between low-skill manual occupations and the average.[63] On the other hand, the measure of overall control over time looks at average leisure, conditions for parental leave, level and gender sharing of part-time work, gender sharing of housework, net costs of child-care, and a measure of employment security.

81

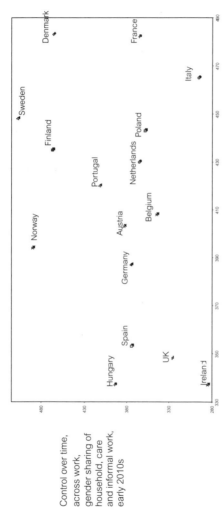

Figure 6. Control over Time, in Work and across Work, Early 2010s

Sources: In work: Index elaborated on the basis of the Fifth European Survey on Working Conditions, 2010; based on task and time control and well-being at work, considering the average and the difference between the average and low-skill manual workers, Table 10a, Column 4.1 and 4.3 in Appendix. Across work: Index based on average annual leisure hours, general and gender share of part-time employment, parental leave length Difference in male/female time for daily informal work, average employment and unemployment tenure; net costs of child-care fees, Table 9, Column 11 in Appendix

Essentially, figure 6 suggests that there is a link between extension of economic security and control of time, and this is mediated through cooperative institutions. The role of humanist policies that have played a key role in Nordic states, where control of time is higher, came about in that context. The Nordic cases show how effective developmental public policy necessarily extends across many policy fields. In these cases, humanist schooling was supported through suppression of ability tests,[64] and the promotion of equal finance for state and private education.[65] In the labour market, support for occupational inclusion took the shape of subsidies for occupationally constructed apprenticeships, extensive subsidized child-care, collective work-time reduction, and 'protected' jobs in place of subsidy for low-wage, or part-time, work.[66] In income support, age-categorical systems like early retirement, and generous support for sabbaticals of various kinds – policies that can be seen as forerunners to basic income – came about in this setting.[67]

The point to take away from this is how support in practice for humanist policies in Nordic states emerged through cooperative practice. The democratic defence of basic income has in this sense already run its experiment: income security administration was most lax – most like a basic income – in the early 1980s in Denmark, at the time when membership of occupational institutions was at its apex. However, history is not sufficient as a guide in imaging our future. In addition, we must be constantly watchful of how the substance and operation of current rules change so that we can assess if it is time to change them. And, if we cannot change institutions by practice, we must try reason instead.

The Competition Economy and the Process of Justice

Basic income is important in reshaping the rules. Processes that deepen inequality and eventually weaken the state and society often initially emerge through institutional changes to the structure of the productive economy. As Piketty has suggested in his work on capitalism, a breakdown of rules (as distinct from changes in education or technology)[68] is responsible for the way in which, since the 1980s, 'super-managers' have been able to set their own wage. To further illustrate, the global share of workers in unions, which help to enforce legal standards, has fallen dramatically: in Germany, from 35 to 18%; in Britain from 50 to 26%; in the US, from 22 to 11%; and, in Mexico, from 24 to 14%, between 1980 and 2013. In Belgium and the Nordic states, the fall was much less, though in Denmark and Sweden there was a reduction from around 78 to 67% in this period.[69]

Rule-loss is a consecutive process. Weakening of social actors' and states' regulatory power has forced governments to play catch-up with the private sector in a race it cannot win. Making the attempt to catch up, states end up generating competition processes within public provision that have no positive end for those who fall behind. Taking education as an example, a growing differential in resourcing between public and private provision,[70] along with the ideology of competition, has spurred states on to generate competition within public sector institutions in an effort to measure up to the market. This is fruitless because public provision has to cover universal risks, whereas the private sector can select.

To exemplify further when formative institutions construct competition or exclusion, as in the case of ability-downgrading in schools, and the sanctions regime in income support, they normalize and justify the inequalities they construct. As in this context a commitment to basic income is a dedication to abating the corroding effect of competition in social relations, taking steps towards basic income is also to mount a defence of the publicness of justice itself, and a way to make it more likely. Illustrating this, a recent British Supreme Court ruling on fees in employment tribunals contained a set of accompanying notes, which can be interpreted as a case against merely retrospective justice, in a way that is relevant to illustrate a basic income's role in forefronting justice. In said notes, the Court went beyond the particular to address the nature and sources of a lack of justice prevailing in the norms and practices of society. For example, in reflecting on a contemporary lack of public understanding of 'the importance of the rule of law', the Supreme Court lamented 'the assumption that ... the provision of those [justice] services is of value only to the users *themselves* and to those who are remunerated for their participation in the proceedings.'[71] In essence, the Court is here saying that wealth and inequality should not be factors in preventing justice, yet the power to purchase, and prevalence of norms of individual interest in matters of justice, have been the outcome of monetizing social relations. Furthermore, in referring to the *vulnerability of* employees to exploitation, discrimination, and other undesirable practices, and the social problems that can result', the judgment affirmed the way '*Parliament has long intervened in those relationships* so as to confer *statutory rights on employees*, rather than leaving their rights to be determined by *freedom of contract*' (paragraph 6, p. 3, emphasis added). Then, what the Court seemingly set out *here* is not just a case against legal fees, but a form of developmental regulation and worker representation. Moreover, the Court warned against a purely contractual framework within the economy, highlighting the responsibility resting on government to positively correct inequalities of power, and affirming the necessarily public character of justice.[72]

Specifically, with regard to effects on *social relations*, the Court noted how lawyers acting in employment tribunals had observed how employers became unwilling to negotiate with employees knowing public justice was unlikely.[73] For example, many lawyers at the time expressed the view that the anticipation of the discouragement to seek justice (there was a 79% fall in claims after the introduction of fees),[74] had encouraged circumvention of norms, a changed attitude to rights of employees, and a disposition against settling disputes pre-emptively.[75]

In all, in bringing to light the social effects of the knowledge of absence of justice, the reasoning accompanying the Court ruling lends force to the case that institutions of permanent, individual security are important for justice to prevail. The absence of effective deterrence sets expectations that abuses can go unchecked. It indicates in a way that is analogous to the humanist defence of basic income the importance of the governing of real security for individuals within the *everyday* economy for supporting the normative force of humanist laws that exist. In the end, a reactionary form of governing – governing to manage crises or the effects of exclusion – generates new states of injustice by individualizing the *process* of attaining justice. Justice in basic subsistence security, and security in labour standards, are similar with regard to the practical importance of justice prevailing, rather than having to be argued for in individual cases. There is in the narrative that accompanies the Court's judgment, a sense of isolation in supporting justice, of lamenting the absence of a society capable of supporting and minimizing the need for court intervention. On the one hand, the Supreme Court stepping in, in the case discussed, can be considered an effective check on government. However, on the other hand, the Supreme Court judgment came into being only because a labour union had brought a case. In the absence of institutions to support justice in an everyday sense, it was justice by chance rather than justice prevailing. Labour unions are weakening and do not represent all employees. This highlights, then, from another perspective, the role of legally permanent economic security in protecting the force of laws already in place. Everyday justice in employment is harder to conceive where an individual's standing is not backed up by independent security. Selection processes in later education and employment are harder to justify when children have not had genuinely open-ended, equal education opportunities or such opportunities do not continue in adult life. With a basic income in place, would unions have been rolled back quite so easily? On this account, basic income may be considered elementary and critical to correct injustice, as well as to *enable* human development freedom and justice to prevail, as well as forestall injustice occurring, and systems corroding.

In summary, in this chapter I have argued that a turn in the last 15 years by states to govern basic income security in a more punitive manner can be interpreted as an outcome of a long-term corrosion of humanist institutions and justice in society. At the same time, as I have also discussed in this chapter, human development justice is hard to construct.

The real issue involved is justice in human time itself. Stabilizing income security payments makes a contribution towards this larger task. A High Court judgment in Britain in January 2019, which established the justice of stable income security payments, further illustrates the issues at stake. This ruling did not refer directly to the justice in stability involved, but to failure to implement a structure of payments that implied it, by reference to ramifications of calculating support within 'a fixed monthly period, known as an assessment period' within Britain's Universal Credit.[76] Hence, the ruling tested and affirmed what has been presumed in welfare policy concerning a regularity principle, the same that ultimately establishes the case for basic income reform. At the same time, arguably, the regularity principle in income support refers to a wider regularity norm within human development justice, concerning stable structures. This was apparent in the material informing the ruling, as witness statements highlighted the pertinence of other regular commitments, to budgeting for household and children.[77] Ultimately, the implication is to suggest the way different economic security structures bind each other: a basic income that is effective for enabling individuals to gain control over the development of their lives is one that is nestled in a wider set of stable human development structures. The defence of basic income in terms of incorporation made in the previous chapter comes into force here, because the way we think of justice standards in social relations is coloured by what actually occurs. Occurrence is a form of social permission. We may notionally subscribe to norms of security in subsistence and justice in social relations, but if we allow their means of attainment to lapse, reality becomes the new standard: it is then up to individuals to *try to reason for justice* to obtain it. When justice is only a remote possibility, it does not prevail. Justice exists when it is embedded in the conditions individuals receive. Justice should act on individuals' behalf. Hence, to the extent that basic income restores the status of individuals in society, it contributes to reverse the force of market contractual norms.

To conclude, in two broad ways, basic income may be a source of reconstituting humanist governance. First, undertaking to implement a basic income properly would demand formalizing or re-formalizing the status of persons as citizens and render unacceptable the current situation whereby many individuals fall behind in developmental processes, as described in this chapter, or fall out of formal society altogether, as described in chapter

1. Second, a provision like basic income may serve to reinforce legal and normative expectations concerning equality in basic developmental processes, referring to laws and practices that already exist or are accepted, thus bringing into view a basic income's broader institutional value for the conception of citizen equality, for effective governance, and for humanist justice.

3

Democratic Development

The case for basic income as greater freedom for individuals discussed in the previous chapter begs a discussion of the governance of development. Consequently, in this chapter I set long-term development policy and rights aspects of basic income together within a broader context of rethinking the relation between different levels of democratic development. I argue that public policy debate has focused disproportionally on the short-term 'cost' of social policy, against the alternative cost of not regulating and taxing better, and the simple question what is the right thing to do. It has also made us forget the most important aspects of basic income, which is about changing the *way* things are done. To consider the consequences, in this chapter I first how a broad case is to be made for basic income in the context of constructing civilized development paths.

Democratic Development

Next, I set out how the institutional perspective on democratic development answers common questions concerning the relation of basic income with the constitution of society and to other transfers, services and technology. Last, I consider lessons we can learn from the occurrence of basic income-like experiments in countries where shared welfare services and occupation economies are more developed.

Democratic Equality and Public Effectiveness

As discussed in chapter 1, the democratic governance case for basic income shares several arguments with libertarian and direct democracy perspectives concerning the status of individuals. However, when it comes to the setting of basic income in the real context of governing society and development, we need a broader account. Notably, a linkage of basic income with individual economy and self-organization is relatively recent. Despite their different political projects, eighteenth-century advocates of an early form of basic income, like Spence and Paine, were both concerned about the wider question of political civilization and the problem of equality in social relations. For Spence, property in land and dividends propped up freedom in social relations: 'The Law does not acknowledge servitude; there can exist only an engagement of care and gratitude between the man who labours and the man who employs him.'[1] Paine viewed raw capitalism as *systemically* exploitative, in which 'The contrast of affluence and wretchedness ... is like dead and living bodies chained together'.[2] In the context of the marketization of development, and the rise in inequality of the last forty years, it is relevant to resituate basic income as part of the enduring challenge to recreate the foundations for civil society.

Contemporary globalization has not led to the spread of knowledge and capability throughout society as marketization theorists promised. Figure 7 shows the trend in the share of world income held by the wealthiest 62 individuals against the bottom 50% of the world population, clearly indicating the rise in concentration since the 2008 financial crisis.

The process of resource concentration and concomitant loss of public regulatory powers has involved a complex set of factors. Across mature economies, corporate taxation rates were cut by a half or a third between the early 1980s and 2015, in the Netherlands from 60 to 16%, in the UK from 52 to 19%.[3] At the same time, the share of resources outside the taxable economy, and thus

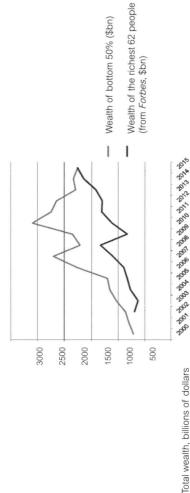

Shifting fortunes of the world's richest 62 individuals against the world's 50% poorest

— Wealth of bottom 50% ($bn)

▌ Wealth of the richest 62 people (from *Forbes*, $bn)

Total wealth, billions of dollars

Source: Oxfam 2016: An Economy for the 1%, p.3.
https://d1tn3vj7xz9fdh.cloudfront.net/s3fs-public/file_attachments/bp210-economy-one-percent-tax-havens-180116-en_0.pdf
Based on Wealth of the bottom 50% from Credit Suisse, Global Wealth Databook 2015. Data on the net wealth of the richest
62 individuals from Forbes' annual list of billionaires.

Figure 7. World Income Concentration, 2000–2015

beyond the measure of GDP, which is the standard basis for gauging how strong public fiscal powers are, rose phenomenally.[4] The IMF has shown that the global size of repackaged credit, as opposed to private sector or real economy credit, grew from around two-thirds of finance in 1980 to almost 90% of finance around 2013.[5]

In this context, it is all too easy to get caught up in annual budget cycles – and to overlook the relationship between policy efficacy and regulatory power – when discussing whether basic income is sensible and affordable. For example, against the annual losses to the UK Treasury from evasion and corporate investment in tax havens, estimated at between £12 billion and £40 billion,[6] the projected annual cost of a universal basic income in the UK, calculated at around £2 billion,[7] as shown in chapter 1, seems no longer based on the kind of fantasy 'money-tree' economics that critics claim.[8] On the other hand, nor can basic income be set outside the wider challenge of improving the regulatory effectiveness of public policy. For example, it is estimated that weak regulation of rents[9] costs the UK Treasury £1 billion per annum in oversized social housing subsidy bills.[10]

The problem of regulatory-effective public spending goes to the heart of the discussion of basic income and social contribution. The IMF has conceded states put too much trust in the market: corporations have reneged on the public's trust by not diverting resources into productive investment.[11] Extraordinarily, here the IMF is admitting that the economic theory behind regulatory policies of the last four decades, which gave corporations more power to structure employment and set wages, was simply wrong.[12] Hierarchical political and economic systems are to blame.[13] Yet, the loss of public power is not only fiscal but institutional and structural. The consultancy firm McKinsey projects that to avoid 'long-term and permanent joblessness' and 'older workers ... drop[ping] out', 'job creation for low-skill workers in advanced economies would need to be at least five times higher'.[14] Yet, states cannot afford, and neither ought they, to target future education and training investments at simply sustaining low-quality employment by 'following the market'. This would only draw states further into the toxic relation with citizens exemplified by sanctions policies. Blanket tax breaks for training do not automatically trickle down to upgrading production structures or improve labour relations. Similarly, in countries with high inequality, such as in Latin America, unstable employment and income insecurity are effectively reduced by targeted policies only up to a point. In

Brazil, massive coverage expansion of income support programmes since 2003 (from less than 10% to now covering over a quarter of the population) contributed to reducing income inequality to 0.51 in 2014, from 0.6 in 1990.[15] Yet, the absolute wealth gap in Brazil grew in this period.[16] Brazil shows the classic political problem faced by high-inequality states, which is that targeting the poorest yields immediate results, but does not build a welfare state. However, as external agencies can harvest measurable outcomes in the short term through targeting the poorest,[17] they tend to advocate slashing universal programmes to favour more targeting.[18]

As discussed previously, in the advanced countries in which inequality is reduced most effectively through redistribution – the Nordic states – this redistribution forms part of a wider incorporation model that is both financed and legitimated by high tax rates across income brackets.[19] This structure supports public finance, but it is enabled by something else: better economic institutions. Nordic states spend a little more, because to achieve the desired regulatory outcome, more spending (in education, employment policy, and care) is needed. The sustained performance of Nordic states in human development terms suggests a very high return to this additional spend, as indicated in figures 8 and 9.

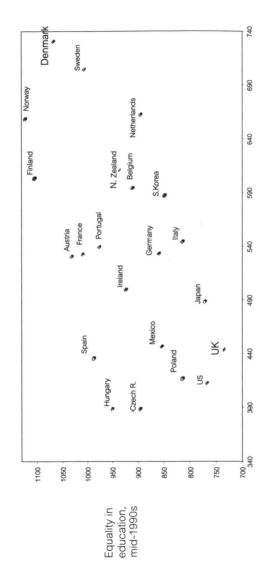

Equality in education, mid-1990s

Sources and calculations: Appendix Tables A3 and A4

Figure 8. Human Development States: Labour Market Returns to Education, mid-1990s

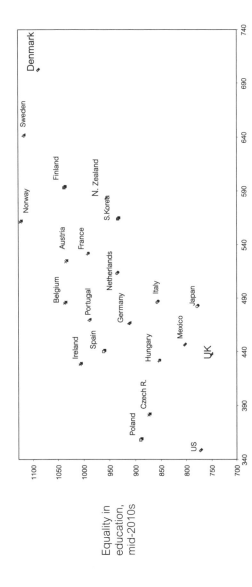

Sources and calculations: Appendix Tables A3 and A4

Figure 9. Human Development States: Labour Market Returns to Education, mid-2010s

The index shown of equality in education includes measures of the level of public expenditure in GDP and in public spending, the level of attained education in the population, share of public spending on tertiary and higher education, the ratio of public to private spending, and the level of equality in resourcing for state and private schools.[20] The index of returns to education measures the difference in the level of returns to education of women with high and median levels of education, covering employment, unemployment, and income differences.[21] Combined, they suggest that countries with more universal coverage of education opportunities generally achieve more equal employment opportunities, yet all countries have seen labour market inequality grow since the 2008 financial crisis.

The comparison of returns to more or less equal education is important to the basic income discussion because it shows that affecting institutions is as important as redistributing income through transfers, or at least both areas of public policy are involved in a positive outcome. Building forms of what I have called occupational citizenship – a right to enjoy stability of and control in occupational life[22] – involves a range of regulatory measures. These measures and institutions involved are crucial in enabling lower levels of both developmental and income inequality.

Arguably, inequality of income and security are jointly behind the poverty in the UK that is estimated to cost the UK treasury £78 billion every year (equivalent to almost three-quarters of the National Health Service budget).[23] At the same time, since the Joseph Rowntree Foundation report citing these figures relies on estimates of 'knock-on' effects of growing up in poverty, the policy implications need to be interpreted carefully. The poor 'falling behind' within education systems, and growing up in households without decent employment income, are also products of institutional factors linked with competitive processes in education that interact with fragmentation in labour market institutions, feeding back into the value of income assistance. Denmark, like the UK and other European countries, has pursued benefit cap policies under recent governments. Still, in 2013, the level of the lowest benefits in Denmark was nearly 2.5 times higher than in the UK.[24] This shows how benefit levels are affected by the overall level of social equality. In this context, the two key objections to basic income – the cost of the programme and the concern that contributions will fall – can be turned around to make a case for a reverse developmental incentive structure, one that begins with stabilizing incorporation mechanisms in society, so as to enable cooperative structures to form.

The difficulty in constructing cooperation in larger societies has been a central theme in modern humanist thought. The philosopher Immanuel Kant emphasized how honour includes keeping promises to others.[25] Relatedly, the political scientist Laurence Whitehead has observed how society 'becoming civil' involves a form of rules individuals in a community are able to obey willingly.[26] In this context, I argue, a stable society relies on a positive interaction between different stable economies, in production, social insurance, and in security in income, housing, services, and human time. Destabilizing one part of the system affects the whole. Moreover, thinking about basic income alongside other democratic projects is of particular importance today, given modern risks linked with progressively becoming excluded *from* society, as discussed in earlier chapters. The German sociologist Ralf Dahrendorf[27] aptly outlined the ubiquitous character of market systemic risk when in the 1990s he revived a term – *anomie* – which Durkheim a hundred years earlier had used to refer to the way competition processes linked with modernity generated *distinctly new* vulnerabilities, as endless striving ('insatiable appetite') separates the self from social bonds and human reality.[28] In illustration, a manifestation of the loss of care in a modern competition economy is the large and growing number of elderly individuals living on their own.[29] Loss of place is also exemplified by the modern vast movements of economic migration, although a rise in homelessness and dependence on food charities suggest that nomadic existences are linked with local economic structures as well.[30]

As an example of the [cooperative character of the] problem of individuals' loss of control in modernity, the philosopher David James has drawn on Fichte's ideas of time as a matter of politics to suggest that capitalism can be viewed as unjust because of the way it divides pressures of work *intensity* unequally.[31] We can extend this to claim modern capitalism is unjust because it divides *stability* unequally.[32] In advanced countries, the young generation is the biggest loser from the abandonment of planned and shared development. The author of the comprehensive Credit Suisse report into global wealth inequality notes, 'We expect only a minority of high achievers and those in high demand sectors such as technology or finance to effectively overcome the "millennium disadvantage"'.[33] Within the current model of income support, retirement may be the first time individuals feel secure – and even now for many in rich nations this is no longer true, given the rising phenomenon of life-time cumulative debt.[34] In this context, whilst basic income does not resolve the debt-creating structure of modern economies, it brings into focus the problem of personification of financial risk, and takes a firm step to begin to address it, including by begging wider regulatory changes needed to convert life necessities into non-mortgageable property.

Arguably, generating the basis for a future stable civil society is the biggest generational challenge of our time. The postwar project was formed around the idea of inter-generational independence and justice: the notion that parents' status should not affect the chances of a new generation. Conversely, the way young people have become increasingly dependent on parents for housing, savings, and inheritance represents the diminution of the public sphere today. The public project itself is at stake, spelling political chaos, the emergence of para-states and economies, and a new politics of envy. After the great recession of 2008, labour fragmentation has seen very low- and high-skill employment grow, yet the majority of the labour force is at risk and youth unemployment has reached 'crisis proportions'.[35]

Democratic Development

Basic Income and State Feasibility

The setting out of the UN's 2030 Sustainable Development Goals (SDGs) highlights a disjuncture that exists today between development objectives and governance capacity around the world. Illustrating this, the way the SDGs set more extensive and life-cycle-related targets, at the same time as state powers to implement such goals have weakened, is deeply ironic. Countries now should not merely end hunger, but improve nutrition and achieve food security. Countries should not just ensure universal primary education, but promote 'inclusive and equitable quality' of education, as well as 'life-long learning for all'. In addition, the UN set out for the first time as explicit goals of government, to foster 'effective, accountable and inclusive institutions at *all levels*'.[36]

The disjuncture between the SDGs' ambition and states' disempowerment highlights the importance of – and potential for – setting the basic income within a broader constructive agenda. States obsessed with short-term savings on social programmes are ceding the power to constitute the citizen, thereby jeopardizing legal structures in the future. Illustrating this, the interest in basic income that exists today is far more general than cautious and partial experimentation by governments sug-

106

gests. All over the world, crowdfunding campaigns have emerged, many led by young activists, some by NGOs and think tanks, and others by corporations. Common to all of these is a shared frustration about the lack of public action in the face of the collapse of market-led solutions to social integration. Motives behind advocacy differ. In the case of a German group of activists who are distributing annual 'basic incomes' to the value of €12,000 per annum from a fund of over €1.5 million raised since 2014, the intention is to demonstrate that the principle of sharing works to generate social trust where states have failed, as hostile income security policies have reduced take-up over the last ten years.[37] Asked about the inherent problems in crowdfunding – for example, such systems do not cover everyone, only those who join, and they are not reliable as financial systems, as they have no central bank propping them up – the reply is that public systems have had a chance and have fallen short.[38] Other alternative initiatives to fund a basic income come from the corporate world, in particular Silicon Valley. An entrepreneurial group heavily involved in blockchain has set aside 'somewhere between 200 and 300 million' dollars for philanthropic causes, and funding a large-scale basic income experiment is a prime contender.[39] Asked if such systems are not prone to capture by criminals and inherently unstable, an entrepreneur staking his candidacy for governing the latest cryptocurrency, EOS, on promoting basic income funding via blockchain, pointed out that several of the existing blockchains are already 'the size of states'.[40] Explaining why he favours universal basic income as a philanthropic goal, he observed, 'I am from India originally, and look at the mess the Indian government is making of social security.'[41] What do these examples tell us? They reveal that the will and the money to fund large-scale basic income experiments are out there, but outside the framework of states. Cynics are right to point out that it is ironic that companies that could pay tax to fund a basic income are prepared to do so on a philanthropic basis. Yet, it is states that need to set the regulatory frame, and initiate the tax.

Hence, I look at the bigger picture, the question is not if states are able or willing to take steps towards basic income, but whether the viability of states may depend on it. We need to ask the classic political science question: who governs? The answer is that the agents who generate and back up security in society govern. Are states prepared to give over power to protect to the new governors of parallel money? Or will states use their regulatory powers to seek a new deal for civil society, by consolidating public property and tax from new sources, as the IMF has suggested? Are we content that a hostile social policy environment makes it rational for ever larger groups in society to seek security in informal structures? The way Bitcoin has become a currency of refugees shows how real opportunity for security locally is a global challenge for states.[42]

In fact, contemporary states have internalized their constraints to such a degree that they have become unable and unwilling to imagine development. For example, to counter bias, and establish *political feasibility* in the terms of received norms, many basic income experiments compel some reciprocity through citizens' services or charitable duties, thereby giving credit to mistaken thinking of the kind I outlined in chapter 1, that is, the thought that we do in fact earn all the basic things we need and receive.

Relatedly, a concern with *psychological feasibility* in the context of basic income experiments is that this identifies particular individuals' mental states as the problem rather than what is generally behind the situation that people are in. Do we really need social experiments to witness that basic status stability and equality are in themselves positive sources of human motivation? Can this not be taken for granted? Imagine a set of speakers coming to debate about basic income receiving different terms in their travel expenses, or in their seating in the debate, depending on what means they have. Immediately, the debate would be distracted by feelings of inferiority or stigma, and the arguments presented would be contaminated by this prior inequality in treatment, which would only make even prior inequalities more evident. The point is, basic income helps to ensure that equality of standing in more specific situations is possible. The philosopher Hannah Arendt's depiction of a democratic setting in terms of equidistant seating at a table springs to mind.[43] This example illustrates how we routinely correct for prior inequalities when we try to produce shared value, whether in the seating in a classroom or in a public debate. A basic income helps protect public reason in all kinds of settings.

Relatedly, an inbuilt problem with the short-term *fiscal feasibility* discourse is that this draws attention to received constraints when we should focus on how institutions like basic income can help construct future capacity for governance and justice. Previous welfare revolutions have not proceeded in this way. Just as in the case of the origination of taxation systems and of treasured modern institutions like the National Health Service, the goal drove the money, not the other way around.

The costs of means-testing are often highlighted in the case for basic income reform. Whether in South Africa, where the economist Pieter le Roux once commented that it cost 40 dollars to pay a villager 100 dollars a month,[44] or India, where it is estimated work schemes cost three rupees to give a person one,[45] or the UK, where historically targeting is estimated to have cost between double and four times more than universal schemes per beneficiary,[46] the problem is universal. Service providers charged with helping individuals into stable employment are also subject to cost-ineffective governance. In Brazil, reliance on six-month contracts forced many training providers, encouraged to forge deep linkages with employer networks, to go bust.[47] Hence, today, the costs of means-testing and franchising the public sector are two sides of the same coin, highlighting how short-termism linked with modern austerity tends against building individual and social capability and cost-coherent policy.

Economy and Democracy

History has shown us that the economic foundations for political democracy shape the scope for inclusive development. The incidence of early land reform in democratization foreshadows the key role in political inclusion basic income can play today. In Nordic states, prior to parliamentary democracy, kings had pursued land redistribution to circumvent aristocratic power, in the process instituting the basis for effective taxation.[48] In turn, this reduced elites' reasons or ability to oppose developmental policies and protections.[49] Similarly, land reform and mass literacy preceded political democratization in Japan and South Korea.[50] Contrastingly, in the case of India, it is claimed franchise extension at the point of independence in 1947 was required to enable governance of a hierarchical society, subsequently cementing social inequality.[51] In Chile, supporting the introduction of democracy after neoliberal reforms required sacrificing the reinstatement of economic rights.[52] Similarly, going back to the early formation of capitalism in Britain, it is argued caution ruled against economic democratization at key junctures. It is claimed that the question of civil economic freedom and equality was sacrificed to enable electoral and other civil rights to be born.[53] The concern of liberal reformers was that 'placing liberty in security' would be 'unattainable in experience', and 'inflame expectations that can never be gratified.'[54] Others have argued that inequalities that consequently prevailed during early capitalism and mass urbanization set out a lasting path of low-skill development within wide segments of society.[55]

Whatever the long-run context, democratization of money institutions and distribution has been key to inclusive development over time. Sandberg describes Sweden in the nineteenth century as the 'impoverished sophisticate'.[56] Widely distributed educational, money and property infrastructure was the backbone behind Sweden's rise from dogged poverty.[57] In the postwar period, a developmental structure of money became more ubiquitous across the developed world. In turn, this structure was inherent in many of the arrangements we think of as civilized economic institutions, including impersonal contracting, diversification of social risk, the ability to receive stable rewards and time schedules for leisure and care through regulated formal employment, and giving women independent resources. Saving, conserving and deferring gratification can be considered the pillars of stable lives and societies. Yet, we should not forget what makes such virtues possible. The assurance of balanced risk – security and the opportunity for regular rewards from different sources – are conditions individuals are increasingly unable to attain today.

Basic Income and Other Benefits

An *intention* to effectively incorporate society should eventually lead to a form of basic income combined with needs-based welfare, because this combination delivers cost and human development effective social security. In this context, a key problem with the roll-out of a new unified payments system (Universal Credit, UC) in the UK has been the way converging means-tests and behaviour conditions in practice (and through targets to limit access) deter uptake within the system. Were the UK or other countries like Finland or Canada – as is being discussed[58] – to adopt a version of UC with less or no conditions – or what would be a form of negative income tax (NIT) – giving people 'back' what they need for subsistence if earnings fall short – this could improve coverage.

Three serious problems, however, would still remain in an NIT scheme. First, a risk with in-effect targeted systems like negative income tax is that behaviour conditionalities may creep back in: the political unity around a shared right that protects encroachment of this kind in a national health service would not exist. Second, tracking fluctuations in incomes will remain costly and prone to error.[59] Third, NIT systems have the inbuilt risk that they simply reproduce and idealize market fluctuations. This points to a more general problem surrounding the legal protection of basic income and the form of public governance more likely to offer it. A devil's deal is one in which basic income supports the structure that generates the insecurity that basic income seeks to abate. Hence, one must be careful about the term 'simplification' in relation to basic income reform. A basic income pursued in isolation or without legal support may be usurped by pre-existing or new forms of dependence. Results from basic income pilots in India, for example, show that cash grants allow indentured labourers to better manage their debts.[60] Yet, in this case – given underlying inequality – dependence remained. In general, new forms of financialized dependence – the use of market rather than public finance to pay for essential goods and services – compounds the exclusions global competition creates. Financialization entails staking a growing share of generalized consumption and investment on repackaged, destabilized debt. Not only does this predictably starve society of long-term private investment, whilst saddling individuals displaced by competition with unmanageable burdens, as too many enter the same race. In addition, as states become insurers of last resort, and public funds are also diverted from long-term investment, states become obligated to seek to divest themselves from insuring society. Ultimately, it is therefore the combination of globalized competition and financialization that explains the rise in more punitive and exclusionary income benefit policies after the 2008 financial crisis. And hence, the fight for the publicness of income security is also a fight for an altered development model. In this context, a positive way to think about basic income as a modern foundation for building new cooperative systems is therefore to envisage the payment as a basic layer within a three-pronged system of human development security based on unconditional and needs-based welfare, public regulation and investment to rebuild occupation economies, and public support for systems of contributions and savings. This foundation model supports the integrity of the elements of basic income – universality, non-mortgageability, permanence, individuality and unconditionality – by enabling institutions of stable inclusion. By consolidating hybrid – social and individual – property in the development and stable use of skills, this model also promotes occupational citizenship within society. In addition, such a system also supports efficient use of resources by ensuring that return for investments in human learning are optimized over the individual life cycle and across society as a whole.[61]

Whilst a moral case for basic income staked on alleviating poverty is tempting in conditions of crisis and rising inequality, such a case is ultimately weak, because it favours charity over equality. Two welfare scholars – Walter Korpi and Joakim Palme – referred to a 'redistribution paradox' to explain how welfare states structured to target the poor do not work politically.[62] In effect, public targeting only plasters over a deeper problem which is high inequality in the private economy. Ultimately, values about public institutions reflect how such institutions are structured: the European Social Survey shows that 65% of respondents in the UK – the most negative attitude by far among OECD countries – think that welfare makes people lazy, compared with 44% in Denmark.[63] The comparably more 'integrated' welfare values of the people in Nordic states[64] can be set against the broader cross-class investment in human development services already discussed.

Basic Income or Services

This raises the question, how is it possible to generate policy coherence (and public norms) around a goal different to austerity? As mentioned, the austerity paradigm has generated a climate in which remedial policies must compete against each other in such a way that an alternative structure of coherence around human development is difficult to conceive. To illustrate, a range of counter-proposals to basic income have emerged in the UK since 2016, in the form of Universal Basic (UB) Services (UBS)[65] and (UB) Infrastructure (UBIIn).[66] Diane Coyle 'call[s] for a guarantee of a Universal Basic Infrastructure – *not income, nor cash, but* access to the transport, communications, and those aspects of health, education, and training that can build "human capital"' (emphasis added).[67] However, the case can be made that basic income *is also* a basic economic infrastructure, as argued. The concern is that pitting opportunity through infrastructure against security in existence fails to address the way current, punitive income security governance undermines human capital investment by excluding and demotivating people just as they face the greatest hardship.

Specifically, the proposition that UBS is a 'logical extension of the widely accepted principle that health and education should be free at the point of use to everyone' is unclear, because UBS is in part a targeted anti-poverty scheme – for example, means-tested free housing.[68] A concern is how a separate new social housing economy might usher in new geographical segregations – divisions which are well known to be critical factors against social mobility. Hence, combining a more universal and regulatory approach is needed: for example, a basic income combined with some regulations of rents and contracts makes it conceivable that people on lower incomes or just on basic income can integrate residentially.

UBS proponents suggest that a common 'shared' benefit of the basic income and UBS is to permit even greater flexibilization of low-wage work.[69] Yet, if enabling greater casualization of work were to be the strategy under a UBS scheme, it could mean individuals continue to be subject to in-work conditionalities and sanctions in relation to necessary wage supplements that draw the state into labour market administration of precarious work. This would then not solve key current problems in benefit systems.

Notably, in the eyes of postwar economists, income security and services were not strangers to, but extensions of, one another. Meade positioned his support for citizens' dividends in 1935 as a continuation of universal services.[70] As Tony Atkinson, Meade's student, remarked more recently, one of Meade's most important – yet ignored – contributions to macroeconomics was the way he lay stress on how 'policy instruments interact with each other'.[71] This insight needs to be rescued when thinking about how to construct equality from the ground up.

Overall, a *societal* basic income model, as promoted here, can be expected to act as an element in enabling cooperative institutions and effective social services and development policies at three levels: individual, policy, and societal. Specifically by supporting a form of *pro-distribution* – distribution *within* individuals' life trajectory and within the economic cycle – basic income acts to stabilize development processes and the economy from within society. Education systems that cease to include after the age of adolescence in effect merely *pre-distribute*. Income security that requires poverty or ill health *redistributes* and creates poverty traps. Instead, basic income can support building a societal system of health constitution and life-long learning. especially if combined with a programme of generating and stabilising new occupation economies, as I examine next.

Democratic Development

Automation and the Future of Work

The democratic argument for basic income also alters our perspective on the impact of new technology under globalization. In a world of growing material and occupational squalor, in which nearly one-third of the world's population suffer malnutrition[72] and 10% lack safe water,[73] the idea that technology-enabled life styles will be possible in the coming decades seems far-fetched. Similarly, the 'end-of-work' argument for basic income is a fairy tale that never comes true. Arguments in the 1930s for basic income based on the sufficiency of our 'technological inheritance'[74] seem bizarre today. Contemporary mass-job-loss predictions tend to focus on the US job market,[75] which has been shaped by a production model that has relied on exporting jobs elsewhere, and on what Esping-Andersen[76] called junk jobs that are more prone to displacement.

Technology does, however, have highly unpredictable impacts, and tends to generate new elites before it generates shared opportunities. A democratic structure of owning technology in common is on the agenda. Some see such a structure linked with paying citizens' dividends,[77] in the form of so-called self-owning machines. Yet such ideas can only work in a public space, through public oversight and ownership. Human organization is the most advanced technology. In every age it is organizational know-how that has pushed civilization forward.[78] Research suggests that a new age of inclusive artificial intelligence (AI) employment will require a combination of social cooperation and more advanced technical skills.[79] Against this, the rise of distant platform working that has occurred surreptitiously is a disorganized use of innovation recognized to debase skills and cause over-intense work schedules and stress. The stability of valued public services is also at stake. For example, in the case of the UK health sector, barriers to hiring permanent staff and avoiding costly agency recruitment, include lack of adequate incentives in the form of student grants and occupational structure.[80]

Combined with development policies, a basic income can encourage settlement in new forms, abating the continual tendency towards intra-regional inequalities. Within a more built-up economic security structure, local cooperative, procurement and service economies – such as in embryonic form in the UK's Preston model – can be better sustained, although one should not be so naïve as to think local procurement can substitute for national investments in the public services occupations that will also be needed. A key role of basic income in this context it to enable settlement.[81] A move to reground individuals geographically is already happening in a fragmented way. Smaller US towns are paying young people to come home, study and take local jobs in what has become known as the new Homestead Act, referring to incentives given to early settlers in the US.[82] Brazilian charities are trying to resettle displaced rural populations and urban dwellers as farmers.[83] Even a small country like Denmark struggles to keep its 407 small islands inhabited.[84] Small-scale introduction of dividends in contained places – like Indian reservations[85] – with less complex stratification structures, evidence the local and intergenerational effects some financial certainty can have.

Governance and Public Norms

Taking a more general view of the development process reveals the significance of democratic development for pushing a rights-based agenda. Just as previous debates about basic income in developing countries have had greater visibility in states or regions with more built-up public sectors and labour unions, such as in South Africa,[86] Brazil,[87] and more lately India, where basic income has been supported by the self-employed women's association (SEWA),[88] it is no accident that partial experiments in basic income have emerged recently in European social democracies like the Netherlands, Finland and Denmark.

Country comparison is useful for bringing out the instrumental factors that drive change. Historically, compared to neighbouring countries, Denmark and the UK had in common a combination of universal systems of health and general taxation-based social insurance and liberal markets in labour. However, liberalization of labour markets in the UK in the 1980s led to a flattening of income security to a low level.[89] In contrast, the still-resilient occupational insurance (OI) system in Denmark pays wage-linked benefits for up to two (previously four) years.[90] There is a case to be made that occupational norms have softened the sanctions regime in Denmark, and shaped the recent push towards basic income experiments. On the one hand, the incentive to self-insure in the OI system diversifies the sources of funding security and improves opportunities for added security. On the other hand, the OI system is linked with training systems, and has contributed to strengthening humanist and egalitarian norms. To illustrate, in a comparison of seven other European countries, the Danish OI system was found to apply the lowest sanctions on voluntary quits, and to operate the most flexible contribution requirements.[91] The error rate in OI sanctioning is low: 4% against 32% in Danish municipalities.[92]

A more developmental form of public and labour market administration has also arguably softened the form of social assistance sanctions in Denmark. For example, legal provisions which mandate that public officials must protect vulnerable persons[93] are a factor in the better health of those sanctioned (e.g. social workers avoid sanctioning individuals who are in poor health).[94]

Moreover, despite a higher rate of sanctions, in the Danish public system sanctions are short – at most one or two days' benefit deduction, and many have focused on 'upbringing': an intention to retain in particular young men within education or training has involved a growing tendency to focus sanctions on this demographic.[95] The education component in sanctions in Denmark is reflected in figures 10(a–c), which show that Denmark increased spending on both administration and training, and then cut back on administration as use of sanctions fell.

Differences in the scope of sanctions is relevant for explaining outcomes. Whereas, by some

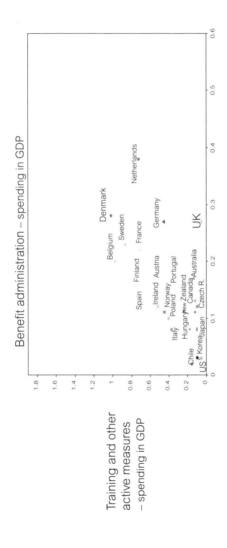

x. Percentage of GDP spent on public benefit administration and placement services, 2007.
Y. Training, employment incentives, supported employment and rehabilitation, direct job creation, start-up incentives, spending in GDP, 2007.
Elaborated from OECD Employment Outlook 2010, Statistical Annex, Table K. Public expenditure and participants stocks in labour market programmes in OECD countries: http://www.oecd.org/employment/emp/43272221.pdf

Figure 10a. Unemployment Systems, 2007

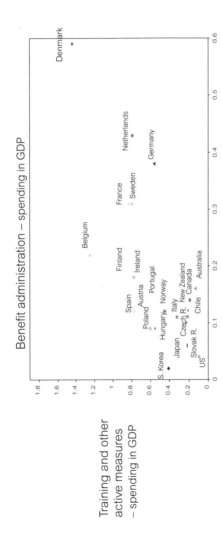

x. Percentage of GDP spent on public benefit administration and placement services, 2010.
Y. Training, employment incentives, supported employment and rehabilitation, direct job creation, start-up incentives, spending in GDP, 2010.
Elaborated from OECD Employment Outlook 2013, Statistical Annex, Table P: Public expenditure and participant stocks in labour market programmes in OECD countries, 2010 and 2011: https://www.oecd-ilibrary.org/docserver/empl_outlook-2013-en.pdf?expires=1547750544&id=id&ac cname=ocid195512a&checksum=23539CE799634F50020BE60759C59B1B

Figure 10b. Unemployment Systems, 2010

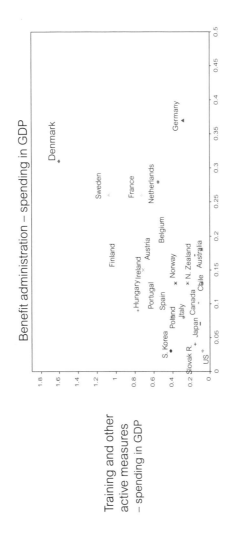

x. Percentage of GDP spent on public benefit administration and placement services, 2014.
Y. Training, employment incentives, supported employment and rehabilitation, direct job creation, start-up incentives, spending in GDP, 2014.
Elaborated from OECD Employment Outlook 2016, Statistical Annex, Table Q: Table Q. Public expenditure and participant stocks in labour market programmes in OECD countries, 2013 and 2014: https://www.oecd-ilibrary.org/docserver/empl_outlook-2016-en.pdf?expires=1547750747&id=id&ac cname=ocid195512a&checksum=168DA56C8078270957702A25DED85420

Figure 10c. Unemployment Systems, 2014

accounts, informalization – defined as non-take-up of benefits – doubled in the UK during the 2010s (see chapter 1), in Denmark less than 1% of people had no public or private income in 2010, and this figure was halved to 0.3% in 2016.[96] In Denmark, sanctions rates peaked in 2011 at a similar rate to the UK (23.9%), but in tandem with reforms to the regime, were brought down to 16.6% by 2014.[97]

In response to public bids to try out new modes of policy delivery, in 2016–17 several Danish municipalities were induced to choose experiments to lift conditionalities as an alternative to sanctions. These experiments are not basic income, but they entail one of the three elements of basic income: namely unconditionality. In one municipality, Kalundborg, rates of enrolment in education or employment programmes reached two-thirds of those eligible – double the national rate – after participation was made voluntary.[98] Moreover, as distinct from the Finnish experiments, in one of the Danish municipalities (Aarhus) the unemployed were given supplementary development grants. According to middle-level managers in the Aarhus experiment of 2017–18, staff were initially hostile to the shift away from compulsion. However, in time, the way social workers were enabled to 'sit down with the citizen as an equal' came to be valued.[99] In the case of Aarhus, social workers pointed out how historical provisions against the assisted owning assets or having savings complicated development programmes. For example, recipients who wanted to start small gardening or delivery businesses were not allowed to own vehicles. In many other cases, recipients wanted to spend development grants on improving basic functioning, by investment in dental treatment, glasses, a driving licence, computer skills, or a bicycle.

In sum, recent partial basic income experiments show that developmental governance is ultimately linked with resistance to punitive governance. In addition, they have brought to light the sorts of problems in existing systems that a basic income would help address. The modest but positive incentivizing effects of lifting conditionalities in Denmark would be amplified under a basic income scheme, because it would also allow individuals to earn, own and save in the future. On the other hand, a key problem with the Nordic and other European experiments to lift conditions on income support is that this does not go far enough towards generating positive incentives.[100] As touched on in chapter 1, policy innovations of different types – including the partial basic income experiments we have seen in mature states recently – remain essentially reactive.

Experimenting with lifting conditions to improve self-motivation may be contradicted by the effect of means-testing: for example, if those receiving funds cannot own or save, what is the incentive to work? Without regenerating investment in occupation economies, will low-skill self-employment be a sub-optimal outcome? Moreover, lifting conditions but not means-tests on basic income grants is like giving half a franchise. A real worry is that partial basic income (lifting conditions but not extending grants universally) will get 'stuck' by cementing targeted approaches, with all the negative implications discussed previously. Because this risk is tied to the austerity agenda that forces narrow policy alternatives, arguing for a full basic income, even if initially a low one – combined with means-tests with additional needs-based support – whilst also pursuing a wider strategy to lower inequality in other economic structures, is essential. Formal status distinctions corrode shared norms, whereas universal inclusion structures help build them. Studies on Sweden have shown that right-wing-leaning occupational groups, like the self-employed, who never embraced the welfare state, came to value *already existing* universal institutions during crisis, suggesting how, in the long run, common systems build trust.[101]

All things considered, universal security structures can be argued to be important not only for justice but also for simply enabling a shared discourse and public understanding, avoiding a regeneration of policy programmes that segregate poor or vulnerable groups from the rest. Basic income has incorporating properties: for example, in a case like the UK, it can support self-employed and other groups at the margins of the welfare state in ways that make their inclusion into mainstream institutions conceivable.[102] A foundation model of basic income is more likely to command support because it can cater to diverse occupational groups. In social democratic states, labour unions are sceptical about basic income given the impact market liberalization has exerted on them. Their leaders want to be assured basic income is not an aid in neoliberals' war against welfare, as the head of one of the biggest unions remarked recently.[103] Prior to the 1990s, subscription to occupation-based unemployment insurance in Denmark covered nearly 90% of the labour force. State-led legislation in the 1990s to promote competition and freedom of choice separated membership of particular unions and unemployment insurance funds, with the upshot that many chose – short-sightedly – to exit the voluntary insurance systems, and subsequently fell directly on basic income support. In this context, adopting three-tier public insurance systems, with basic income as the foundation for publicly assisted mutual insurance and stronger occupational policies, could quell concerns unions have about existing welfare arrangements and unions' roles in supporting them.

At the same time, a growing divide is emerging between the assisted and insured working class in Nordic states. It takes some convincing to enable the assisted poor to see in basic income not only their own salvation, but a means to make existing civic structures more inclusive. For example, some basic income advocates are unhappy that the OI system is not a flat system, like the basic income is. Proposals in Nordic states to privatize unemployment insurance in order to transfer public funds to pay for a basic income,[104] is symptomatic of what is at stake. Yet, another way of looking at it is to say that basic income and OI – which protects earnings for a time – represent two complementary ways of supporting personal control over destiny. Whilst the old OI institutions pay out more to higher earners, the latter also contribute more, and crucially public regulation and subsidy ensure there is both a benefit ceiling and floor. Without public subsidy of the system, private 'risk premiums' would price out the old, sick and low-paid from enjoying the benefits of additional unemployment insurance. Hence, it is important to make the case that the OI and basic income together make a stronger economic security structure.

Ultimately, it is rising inequality that poses the biggest threat to society and basic income as a democratic idea. There is a risk today of the basic income debate being caught up in a new form of market fatalism, by making security in jobs rather than unstable jobs the problem basic income seeks to address.[105] The notion of building an alternative social movement of the dispossessed as basic income creates a 'big strike fund' – as sometimes argued – underestimates how individuals' power is protected by institutional gains. In the end, attempting to turn the old so-called 'occupational' movement into a 'precariat' movement supported by basic income is to settle for less. Highlighting how basic income supports democratic institutions and actors in civil society – many of whom may be hostile to the idea as it has been presented in the past – is a challenging task. However, it is increasingly important as a range of new populist parties see in basic income a way to radically simplify governance through a flat tax, a single transfer model of welfare, full nationalization of money, and – in some cases – keeping foreigners out. A broad democratic defence of basic income is necessary to stake a middle course between the linked extremes of financial opulence and populist nationalism. Hence, I agree with the concern that a flat income security and tax system are likely to drive down public finance and solidarity,[106] but not that this is a case against basic income as such. Basic income is best viewed in the end as a small if crucial part of a larger fiscal and social pact.

Human development, freedom and justice demand a new social settlement, in the form of common property and citizenship in economic stability and a life of occupation. In place of attempting to manage market exclusions through individual policy instruments, governments need to focus on building stable inclusion ground up, through concomitant promotion of stable investment in occupation economies, and the separate stability of basic income and services.

An alternative to managing market exclusions through individual policy instruments is to encourage contribution through a combination of basic income, welfare and infrastructure on the one hand and the development of occupational citizenship on the other.

Overall, looking at the current juncture in global development, we can surmise how the viability of basic income and locally and globally coherent development policy are closely connected. The global character of the debate about basic income carries in this context opportunities as well as risks. The risks are linked with the constraint that justifies the project. History suggests that economic reforms are often politically difficult to implement without an external constraint. This presents a difficult scenario for basic income reform. For example, it is tempting to position basic income as a backstop that justifies or props up the global market – or its opposite in the form of a full nationalization of development. However, a concern is that either course sells basic income at a democratic discount. For example, if appeal is made to external threats or support systems (e.g. automation or blockchain), this presents states' current impotence as inevitable.

Whichever way you look at it, a case for basic income in terms of a defence of the public realm itself makes most sense. Although basic income does not require a high level of social equality to come into being in theory, in practice the supportive funding and values needed to sustain basic income depend on substantive forms of social equality. Social equality tends to be bound up with developmental policies and humanist practices and norms. Consequently, a public case for basic income needs to be grounded in two forms of respect: for civic equality, and for human development. It is not enough to justify basic income in terms of injustices being perpetrated within capitalism because this can generate responses that are in other ways liberty-negating and merely generate a moving and slippery target. For example, proposals to give allowances only to certain income groups does this. The argument that there is not enough suitable employment is also relevant but not sufficient either. In this case, justice presumably suffices if employment opportunities are available, which then might justify the continuation of sanctions. In turn, sanctions generate an immediate justice case for basic income in terms of disproportional treatment of those who are vulnerable. But this again might justify sanctions, if we were only prepared to strip the rich of their money, and impose sanctions on them. It seems, then, we can only object to sanctions and advocate basic income at the same time on broader humanist grounds, demanding not only equal concern for others, but equal respect in terms of human development. This being so explains how the case for basic income is tied up with the case for democracy and for a form of economic development that is grounded in humanist justice.

Conclusion

The Life of a Gentleman

'The question is not whether all men will ultimately be equal – they certainly will not – but whether progress may not go on steadily, if slowly, till, by occupation at least, every man is a gentleman.'

Alfred Marshall, 'The Future of the Working Classes', lecture to the Cambridge Reform Club, 1873, quoted in T.H. Marshall, 1950, *Citizenship and Social Class*, p. 4

'The unified civilisation which makes social inequalities acceptable … is achieved by a *progressive divorce between real and money incomes*. This is, of course, explicit in the major social services, such as health and education, which give benefits in kind without any ad hoc payment. In scholarships and legal aid, prices scaled to money incomes keep real incomes relatively constant, in so far as it is affected by these particular needs. Rent restriction, combined with security of tenure, achieves a different result by different means. So, in varying degrees, do rationing food subsidies, utility goods and price controls. *The advantages obtained for having a larger money income do not disappear, but they are confined to a limited area of consumption.*'

T.H. Marshall, 1950, *Citizenship and Social Class*, p. 81, emphases added

In the second passage above, T.H. Marshall – writing at the time of the formation of the NHS in England – set out how a regulatory approach to human development is necessary for substantive equality – citizenship as membership of a community – as he defined it. Yet, also apparent is how he saw regulation to promote protected spaces as a basis for freedom. For Marshall, value in money was predicated on shared institutions on account of how freedom emerges from conditions in which individuals do not have to negotiate to obtain goods such as low-cost amenities, occupations, and justice. Moreover, for T.H. Marshall, as for Alfred Marshall, in the first quote above, time and core activities – having an occupation – were especially valuable freedoms. Real social progress involved thinking about how those might also become protected spaces for all.

Conclusion

A key concern motivating the democratic case for basic income is social costs linked with excessive competition. It is hard to conceive of individuals having control of time, if society does not. The faster competitive processes in society are, and the less accountable developmental commitments to employment or services are, the more participation in activities depends on stretching beyond human limits. A society of explorers – individuals able to stay, looking out for adventure – is different from a society of nomads, forced to be on the move.

The Life of a Gentleman

'All this had been planned and planted a century and a half ago so that, at about this date, it might be seen in its maturity.'
Evelyn Waugh, *Brideshead Revisited*, p.13

The sense in which a gentlemanly state was imagined in Marshall's time is captured in the above quote by Evelyn Waugh, in which his novel's core character recalls the idyllic settings of home and education, proffered by the country estate and the timeless university. Waugh evokes how these were both predicated on – and derived their value from – the ways in which they were a product of long-term planning, and acquired a maturity and immutability as a result of the absence of the crushing forces of competition and change. The self-possession of Waugh's character of Sebastian is framed by a form of order in his setting that had an importance only time – a sense of belonging to something greater – could give it.

The question here is not the undoubted wealth that grounded opportunity in this case, but what the opportunity comprised in the form of a developmental trajectory, sheltered from competitive forces. The very object of elite education is to in effect guarantee a good outcome, and working backwards to achieve it. By contrast, students in state education governed to track competitive performance of schools are exposed to a constant frame of mass competition that elite students are protected from. Perceiving such problems, Marshall presented the structure of education as an enduring cooperative challenge, noting how even seemingly specific matters, such as small class sizes, and teaching without ability stratifications, were necessary for constructing civilized states.[1] Nordic states have to a greater degree mimicked the orientation of private schools, through a developmental design of civic education, thus without the basis of class distinction instilling in a whole people the sense that values of individuality and social belonging are not mutually exclusive.

Although basic income cannot shape education directly, it can contribute to erasing social distinctions linked with insecurity and lack of status. Basic income is a part of constructing citizenship as a 'developing institution' of different component parts, as Marshall saw it.[2]

The point is, for Marshall, rights had meaning in so far as they assembled a state: the civilized life and the civilized condition. Individuals' freedom and society's institutions were recognized as joint constitutive. In this context, basic income advocates need to resist the capture of this discourse by a modern love affair with subsidiarity, the idea that governing can be simply understood – or is constructed through – individuals' agency and preferences. Ultimately, sanctions regimes against which basic income is rightly pitted are the end-point of over-compartmentalized governing that contradicts commitments to welfare in systems of health and schooling.

If basic income is a good, because secure incorporation in society is conducive to cooperative institutions and inclusive growth, then states in which stability of developmental institutions has public priority are good states. The point of basic income is not that individuals can or ought to construct their own social positions, because this is a fictitious notion in an in reality connected world. Hence, the question is not what we shall shed to fund a basic income (even less a high basic income), but what we shall jointly construct to enable stable, functional, social institutions. It is pointless to stake the debate about basic income on whether generating a stable income infrastructure is sufficient for welfare or for individuals living without society, as the libertarian discourse encourages, and the ideology of austerity, in which current debates about basic income is conducted, extends. The polemic about basic income versus alternatives, or its precise behavioural impact, is not the right framework for judging if an institution is good. We do not argue for universal health care or education on the burden of proof that these individually can allow people to lead independent lives, but whether in conjunction with other institutions, and against the alternatives, they contribute to good social outcomes.

So, this raises the question, how should we think constructively about basic income in the context of democratic and welfare state evolution? Four intentional features of governing – *developmental orientation, low social inequality, publicness,* and *diversification* of social security – interact.

Conclusion

It is important to make a case for a democratic constitution of basic income partly as it is connected with enabling the public realm in general. Besides facilitating a more incorporated structure of tax contribution, a sustainable public sector will depend on states' capacities to tax new economies and physical and digital assets, or to bring a share of those into common ownership for lease or cooperative governance. There is a real chance that otherwise truncated forms of partial and informal basic income security will emerge outside the framework of the public sector, linked to commercial finance and interests, further weakening the public realm, and allowing informal coercive networks to arise in the shadows. Democratic distribution is needed for three forms of public investment: into common regulation and development projects; into human development services and occupations, including education, health and housing constitution, and environmental conservation; and into individual economy. These three democratic distributions are mutually dependent. Policies in individual sectors cost less and are more efficacious in terms of human development, when public capacity in other services is also developed. Coordinating human work in occupation economies will continue to be important because this expands skills, protects formalised and shared knowledge, and critical public culture. The fiscal trade-off debate is a false economy, considering how leading through the use of incentives rather than costly exclusion can improve policies' design and combined effectiveness. Hence, countries need to plan for more coherent institutions of human development. Therefore, whilst I agree with Van Parijs's classic statement that basic income can become progressively developed in the form of a 'a well-embedded gradual lifting of the floor' through individual property in income,[3] it is clear that the real value of this floor will not in fact increase without forming part of a set of systemic changes, in which public investment in, and coordination of, skills development, care, and production, are central.

In sum, as argued in this book, the humanist democratic case for basic income emphasizes the political stability and institution-building properties, as well as the civic morality, entailed in basic income reform. Accordingly, in chapter 1, I discussed how the democratic conception of basic income contests the way fragmented claim-making in social policy activates and implicates the state in chain-connected processes of cumulative advantage and disadvantage involved in marketized society. A person failing to realize one claim, e.g. to highly conditional income assistance, or increasingly rationalized public housing, is excluded from other claims and opportunities arising from income status. The compartmentalization of the public sector in these processes dissipates public responsibility. Therefore, a wider re-democratization of the state is at stake in basic income reform.

As further elaborated in chapter 2, by thus bringing into focus the role of civil rights formation in developmental justice and liberty, the humanist democratic case for basic income entails a different orientation to process theories of democracy and market justice. In placing emphasis on enjoying as distinct from actioning rights, the humanist case reiterates the importance of civil rights and equality in relation to political and economic competition at a time of rapid structural change.

In continuation of this, chapter 3 further explored how the civic democratic conception of basic income also therefore entails an altered development governance model. Evidence that well-being and control of activities vary systemically across polities shows that the scope for different states of being is deeply affected by the governance of developmental institutions, being the rules that shape settlement, education, work and care in a society. The moral logic involved in one developmental institution – like public education, or income support – is infectious. Hence, if a basic income may be only a small element in governance, the step this reform entails towards a civic form of income security may play a pivotal role in system dynamics.

Hence, last, the humanist democratic case for basic income focuses attention on a broader set of political choices. One must be conscious of a wider battle of justification emerging through the vehicle of debate about basic income reform. If basic income has a strong democratic heritage, the idea has also been viewed as a platform for incorporating financial globalization, hence giving sustenance to an ultimately unstable economy.[4]

The basic income project today is the birth-child of a new age of need and search for justification, where rightful hope of the dispossessed blends with the cynicism of the powerful. A populist politics of basic income – linked with projects of parallel economy or a world without work – seamlessly weaves distant narratives together, but at a potential cost of reason and prudence. Platform capitalists making common cause with the sanctioned unemployed against the institutions of regulated employment and stable occupation economies spell the risk of selling basic income at a democratic discount in capital letters.

Hence, one must be careful not to put basic income to the service of a politics of rescue. Good ideas are seized in troubled times. Yet, proclamations of right ring louder in a hollow chamber. Like the plaques calling for respect for racial equality in elevators of public buildings in one of the world's most racialized cities, São Paulo, standalone declarations announce a lack of public capacity. Specifically, I have argued that it is a mistake to position basic income as a singular answer to the insecurities inherent in globalization.

Ultimately, it is the level of civic development of society that gives individual rights substance: it is practical commitments to human security – their careful crafting in law, institutions, and public planning – that determine whether equality is kind or cruel. Giving normative priority to human development sequences and schedules entails casting basic income as a contribution to establishing human development justice. Thus conceived, the life-long security structure entailed in basic income subsistence sets out the value of settlement through other institutions, in the form of stability in housing and occupation. At the same time, basic income does not complete or necessarily enable that settlement, even when it suggests what might be necessary to it, in the form of a large and secure public domain, and an active state. Hence, the packaging of basic income does matter. Basic income can form a part, but not the whole, of a scheme of human development justice and public incorporation. The context in which basic income is being debated today therefore cannot be ignored. A simple flattening of basic income security is not progressive in a world of fracturing employment and rising inequality. A basic income can ameliorate the effects of platform capitalism, yet also restore the distant mode of working involved. A flat distribution ultimately is a cruel form of justice because it absolves society from caring about individuals' fate. In this context, safeguarding the public sector itself – with all it represents of potential for extending the kindness of affectionate ties beyond a small circle – is key not only to finance a basic income sustainably, but to make it progressive.

The contemporary push to test effects of elements of basic income has contributed to bust two forms of myth: about presumed moral hazard entailed in shifting from a control to an incentive model of basic security, and about basic income transitions as a stand alone transformative remedy. Figures released in February 2019, concerning the results of the first year of the Finnish experiment run between 2017 and 2019, to test the effects on 2,000 unemployed of lifting conditions on a share of their income support, are revealing of the multifactorial setting which shapes senses of well-being and occupational inclusion.

As I noted in chapter 2, occupational motivation and well-being are a product of sets of security: the effect of income security on motivation and behaviour (separately) will depend on other factors, e.g. family status, housing security, levels of education, employment stability and occupation opportunities.[5] The Finnish experiment tested the behaviour of unemployed individuals who still faced uncertainty if taking work in regard to the status of other family and housing benefits, which they were receiving.[6] Moreover, the experiment was not combined with changes to employment policy or opportunities. It did not explore impacts within a genuinely universal constituency. Significant employment effects thus were never to be expected. However, beneficiaries were aware that they formed part of a move to lessen benefit conditionality. The experiment held out the promise that conditions within the benefit system might be lessened and hence greater autonomy of recipients was in principle valued. This helps account for the stronger results, which show up in the evaluation of bureaucracy, and the sense of support for incentives. The results suggested small but significant differences in self-reported stress and experience of good health, the latter at 56% among those in the experiment, versus 46% in the control group. However, it is apparent even from the crude data published to date that the most significant difference between the test and control group concerned aspiration and perception in areas more directly relevant to the specific administrative changes that were tested. For example, self-reported senses that financial incentives had increased and bureaucratic barriers to work had fallen, at 68% and 57%, respectively, among the treatment, and 42% and 37%, respectively, among the control group, comprised the statistically most significant results. These findings affirm both the limitations and the promise connected with so-called basic income experiments: limitations, because responding to aspirations raised, such as in Finland, a greater reported desire among the treatment group to move into full-time from part-time work, depends on other factors to support occupational development; yet promise, in evidencing significant positive health and motivational impacts from even small changes in benefit status.

How radical is basic income in liberal terms? It is not very radical when we consider we already assume constant individual economy as a value the public has to protect. A particular risk in presenting basic income as radical is to make it incumbent on governments (and basic income advocates themselves) to 'test' it. Let us instead consider the case that a basic income does not require behavioural experiments for its defence. Here history seems to be on our side. Behavioural tests or short-term fiscal viability studies were not the most significant factors in the development of health care or schooling within the welfare state. Why should the case for basic income be different? Setting basic income reform in a broader institutional and democratic context, defined by recognizing the problem of fundamental human equality, gives to the debate about basic income a humanist democratic defence that is due.

Appendix

Table A1. Structure of Cooperative Public Finance: Public Revenue Scores and Levels

	Total tax revenue as % of GDP 1:1975, 2:2000, 3:2009, 4:2015				(5) a.1975-2000, b.2000-2015, c.1975-2015			(6)		(7)		(8)		9	(10)		(11) a 2000 b2009 c 2016/7			(12) a 2000 b 2009 c 2016/7			(13) a 2000 b 2009 c 2016			(14) Statutory Corporate Income Tax Rate a 1982, b 1994, c 2000, d 2007, e 2010 f 2016/7						(15) Corporate Tax Revenue as a % of GDP a 1965, b 1982, c 1995, d 2000, e 2007, f 2010						16 a 1982-2000, b 2000-2015		17 Public Revenue Score	
	1	2	3	4	a	b	c	6a	6b	7a	7b	8a	8b	9	10a	10b	a	b	c	a	b	c	a	b	c	a	b	c	d	e	f	a	b	c	d	e	f	a	b		
Den	37.0	46.9	45.2	46.6	127	99	120	62.7	1.0	62.1	1.0	55.8	1.2	89	496	492	32	25.0	22.0	40.0	45.0	42.0	59.2	58.8	54.8	40.0	35	32	26	25.0	22.0	1.4	1.1	2.3	3.2	3.8	2.4	2.6	291	81	487	436
Fin	36.1	45.8	40.9	44.0	127	91	122	59.8	2.1	55.0	1.8	58.9	1.8	96	491	485	29	26.0	20.0	29.0	40.5	43.1	62.0	40.5	43.1	29.0	26	29	27	26.0	20.0	2.5	1.5	2.2	5.7	3.9	2.0	2.2	380	39	412	398
Swe	38.9	49.0	44.1	43.3	126	88	111	55.4	1.5	56.5	1.5	60.1	1.5	103	491	487	28	26.3	22.0	28.28	28	28	58.0	48.2	46.6	51.0	28	28	28	26.3	22.0	1.6	1.7	2.6	3.7	8.8	2.8	3.0	231	81	445	410
Nor	38.8	41.9	41.2	38.1	109	91	98	55.3	2.6	47.8	1.6	46.9	1.6	85	432	427	25.0	28.8	28.8	-0.1	28.0	28.8	60.0	48.6	48.6	39.0	28	28	28	24.0	24.0	1.1	7.2	3.7	8.8	11.8	4.5	1.7	122	51	413	365
Ger	34.3	36.2	36.1	36.9	105	102	108	53.8	1.8	47.5	6.3	47.5	5.5	88	443	427	30.2	31.1	26.4	26.4	60.9	48.6	48.6	52	42	39	39.0	15.8	2.5	1.8	1.0	1.8	2.2	1.3	4.0	3.1	100	94	417	319
NL	38.2	37.2	35.4	37.8	97	103	99	60.0	1.8	50.2	1.2	52.7	1.4	87	459	456	35.0	25.5	25.0	35	35	26	55.5	35.0	26.2	48.0	35	35	35	2.9	3.1	4.0	3.2	n/a	2.7	138	68	458	374
Bel	38.8	43.5	44.4	44.8	112	103	115	65.7	2.3	59.4	1.0	58.4	1.0	114	498	472	40.34	33.0	33.0	43.9	51.8	50.0	40	39	35	35	2.3	3.3	1.9	2.0	2.3	3.1	3.5	2.5	3.4	155	110	445	447
Swi	22.5	27.4	27.0	27.9	122	101	124	44.0	3.6	41.1	3.3	41.7	3.5	95	405	395	25	21.2	21.1	8.5	8.5	1.3	1.7	2.2	2.4	3.0	141	125	429	266
Aus	36.4	42.1	41.0	43.5	116	103	120	42.6	2.3	43.7	2.1	55.0	24.7	117	501	460	34.25	26.0	25.0	25.0	43.8	43.8	50.5	47.0	34	34	32	25.0	25.0	1.1	1.4	2.0	1.4	1.7	2.3	182	115	390	170
Fra	34.9	43.1	41.3	45.5	123	106	130	49.9	2.8	49.8	2.8	55.1	14.8	80	517	473	48.87	34.43	34.43	36.4	40.8	44.0	55.9	64.4	50.0	50	35	38	37	2.0	3.0	2.0	3.0	1.4	2.1	136	70	434	326
Spa	18.0	33.4	30.0	33.8	186	101	188	48.0	4.3	43.0	2.4	45.0	2.4	96	436	429	35.30	35.0	30.0	30.0	52.7	42.3	34.0	37	35	33	1.2	1.7	3.0	1.4	4.7	2.2	2.4	250	80	364	330
Por	19.8	31.1	29.9	34.5	164	111	183	46.6	3.4	48.4	4.6	61.3	16.0	132	530	481	37.27	25.0	25.0	25.0	51.4	41.2	49.2	50.0	40	32	28	29.5	23.5	2.9	3.3	3.7	3.2	3.3	2.8	3.1	97	75	373	312
Ita	24.5	40.6	42.1	43.3	166	107	177	46.4	3.6	50.7	3.2	48.8	9.8	105	484	460	37.5	27.5	12.5	12.5	44.9	36.6	46.4	40.0	53	37	32	27.5	27.5	1.8	2.9	1.8	3.3	2.8	2.2	2.1	49	86	389	324
Hun	44.8	38.6	39.2	39.4	86	102	n/a	68.5	0.9	62.0	0.8	33.5	0.0	50	374	374	18.20	19.0	15.0	15.0	40.0	46.7	40.0	n/a	18	na	4.5	n/a	1.2	2.8	2.2	1.9	52	360	318	309
Cze	32.0	32.3	33.5	33.1	88	103	n/a	68.5	2.5	62.0	0.4	33.5	0.4	77	374	372	33.5	32.0	15.0	15.0	33.5	41.4	31.1	na	31	na	6.1	4.3	3.2	5.0	3.6	36	71	314	286
Pol	34.0	32.9	31.4	32.1	97	96	n/a	41.5	3.5	34.9	2.8	38.8	2.1	93	402	395	30.19	19.0	19.0	19.0	34.3	34.4	44.0	n/a	na	3	na	6.6	2.7	2.4	2.8	1.7	44	135	274	252
Slo	33.6	28.9	32.3	33.6	85	96	94	39.7	7.9	29.9	0.5	35.1	3.7	84	382	371	24.12.5	15.0	0.0	0.0	39.7	50.5	44.0	40	19	29	na	5.9	3.0	2.8	2.7	2.6	30	28	382	322
Ire	27.9	30.8	27.4	23.6	110	76	85	50.5	1.0	50.2	7.9	52.0	2.0	101	398	371	24.12.5	12.5	12.5	44.0	41.0	51.0	57.4	48.4	57.1	50.0	40	24	12	2.3	1.6	3.4	2.4	2.7	3.6	225	75	382	322
UK	34.2	32.8	31.5	32.5	96	94	94	48.0	1.3	51.0	1.3	47.0	4.1	118	296	284	21	28.0	20.0	20.0	20.0	44.5	46.0	45.1	52.0	34	30	30	3.7	2.3	3.4	2.5	2.4	2.5	95	71	403	309
US	24.6	28.2	23.0	26.4	115	94	107	48.0	8.8	43.2	8.6	48.6	8.0	80	344	344	39.39	39.1	38.6	38.6	49.4	56.3	65.6	49.4	35	40	35	39	2.9	2.4	2.2	3.0	2.1	2.2	110	100	308	387
Australia	25.4	30.4	25.8	27.8	120	91	109	48.5	1.2	46.5	2.8	49.0	2.2	101	423	416	34.30	22.0	23.1	27.1	48.5	46.5	39.0	34	34	32	2.7	4.2	6.2	4.2	6.8	n/a	4.7	230	76	374	338
NZ	27.5	32.5	30.3	32.8	118	101	119	49.5	4.5	38.0	1.5	33.0	1.2	67	366	362	34.30	28.0	30.0	33.0	38.0	33.0	46.0	33	33	34	2.6	5.0	4.2	5.0	3.3	4.4	154	110	350	304
Jap	20.4	26.6	27.0	32.0	130	120	157	49.5	4.5	38.0	1.7	33.0	4.0	114	498	472	41.39.5	43.6	20.3	10.0	30.0	66.7	45.6	30.0	30	30	na	4.2	4.2	4.8	4.2	2.4	3.2	67	123	387	294
SK	14.9	21.5	23.8	25.3	144	118	170	43.4	5.4	38.5	3.2	43.2	4.0	100	423	410	31.24.2	20.29	35.4	44.0	46.3	51.0	na	na	28	na	1.9	2.2	3.0	4.0	3.7	3.2	158	107	219	295
Mex	14.5	13.6	3.6	7.4	94	105	n/a	42.9	48.6	29.7	4.1	35.0	26.6	82	344	259	30	28.0	0.0	17.3	35.0	28.0	42.0	na	na	30	na	1.7	1.7	n/a	2.0	3.3	100	194	223	214
Chile																																									

Column 5: Total tax revenue as % of GDP, earlier year as 100.

Column 6 - 8: a: Top marginal tax rate, b: Multiple of average wage where sets in.

Column 9: Top marginal tax rate, earlier year as 100.

Column 10: a: $(4*3)+(5b)+(8a*3)+(9)$, b: $(4*3)+(5b)+(8a*3)+(8b*3)+(9)$. Column 11: Corporate income tax on distributed profits. Column 12: Net statutory tax rates on dividend income (shareholder). Column 13: Overall personal income tax and corporate income tax rates on dividend income. Column 16: Corporate tax revenue as % of GDP

Public revenue score (column 17): A: $A(2*4) + (5a/10) + (6a*2) - (6b*10) + (13a*2) + (14c) + (15d*2) + (16a/20)$. B $(4(*4) + (5b/10) + (8a*2)) - (8b*10) + (13c*2) + (14f) + (15*2) + (16b/20)$. Source: Elaborated from OECD Tax revenue statistics.

Table A2. Public Spending on Human Development

Column group legend

- **(1A)** General public expenditure in GDP, (a) 1970, (b) 1980, (c) 1990, (d) 2000, (e) 2005, (f) 2009, (g) 2015*, (h) Trend to 2015, 2000 as 100
- **(1B)** Public social expenditure in GDP, (a) 1990, (b) 2000, (c) 2007, (d) 2014*, (d) Trend to 2014, 1990 as 100
- **(1S)** Score = G1 G2
- **(2A)** Public expenditure on education in GDP, (a) 1995, (b) 2007, (c) 2011, (d) Trend to 2011, 1995 as 100
- **(2B)** Public expenditure in on education in % of public expenditure, (a) 1995, (b) 2007, (c) 2011, (d) Trend to 2011, 1995 as 100
- **(2S)** Score = G1 G2
- **(3)** Training, job creation, and supported employment - public spending (i) 1995/6, (ii) 2006, (iii) 2013, (iv)a Trend to 2006, 1995/6 as 100, 1995/6 as 100, (S) Trend to 2013, 2006 as 100, (S) Score = (ii*200)+(iii/10); sub: (i) (ii) (iii) (iva) (ivb) (S) G1 G2
- **(4)** Public spending on child-care as % of GDP, (i) 1998, (ii) 2005, (iii) 2011, (iv)a Trend to 2005, (iv)a Trend to 2011, 2005 to 2011, (S) Score = 100, (S) Score = (ii*150)+(iv/20); sub: (ii) (iii) (iva) (ivb) (S) G1 G2
- **Column 5** Score = $(1S + (2S^2) + 3S + (4S^2))$ G1 G2

Country	1A a	1A b	1A c	1A d	1A e	1A f	1A g	1A h	1B a	1B b	1B c	1B d	1S G1	1S G2	2A a	2A b	2A c	2A d	2B a	2B b	2B c	2B d	2S G1	2S G2	3 i	3 ii	3 iii	3 iva	3 ivb	3S G1	3S G2	4 ii	4 iii	4 iva	4 ivb	4S G1	4S G2	C5 G1	C5 G2
Den	42.9	53.6	57.0	52.7	51.2	58.6	55.7	106	25.0	26.1	30.1	120	283	306	7.3	7.8	8.7	115	12.2	15.4	15.2	125	97.4	114.4	1.67	1.57	1.82	93	116	343	376	0.7	0.8	2.0	114	250	111	313	1043	1537
Fin	31.9	40.6	48.1	49.3	56.1	57.7	n/a	120	23.8	24.9	31.0	130	266	318	6.8	5.9	6.8	100	11.0	12.5	12.2	111	89.6	90.7	1.54	0.76	1.01	49	133	313	215	0.8	0.7	1.1	86	157	124	173	1006	1060
Swe	n/a	n/a	53.6	52.7	46.3	50.4	n/a	94	28.5	20.8	28.1	98.6	291	277	7.1	6.7	6.8	96	10.7	12.7	13.2	123	92.7	92.2	2.10	1.32	1.35	63	102	426	280	0.7	0.6	1.6	86	267	109	253	1120	1247
Nor	39.1	47.9	44.5	42.0	47.5	48.6	n/a	116	21.9	25.2	22.0	100	233	260	7.9	6.7	8.7	110	15.5	16.4	14.9	96.1	105.8	112.2	1.01	0.58	0.56	57	97	208	122	0.3	0.5	1.2	167	240	53	192	759	990
Ger	39.1	47.9	44.5	44.8	46.2	47.5	43.9	99	21.4	25.2	25.8	121	244	249	4.6	4.5	5.0	109	8.5	10.3	11.0	129	71.4	72.9	1.20	0.60	0.67	50	112	245	145	0.0	0.1	0.5	100	500	20	100	672	740
NL	41.7	55.3	54.8	41.8	42.3	51.4	45.5	108	25.6	20.1	24.7	96.5	239	250	5.1	5.9	5.6	108	9.1	11.7	11.9	131	72.5	83.2	1.22	1.20	0.94	107	78	235	196	0.1	0.9	100	900	25	180	n/a	669	974
Bel	n/a	n/a	49.1	51.4	54.2	54.0	n/a	110	24.9	26.1	30.7	123	270	301	5.8	5.9	6.5	112	12.1	12.4	12.2	101	80.8	87.9	1.16	1.06	0.72	91	68	219	151	0.1	0.2	0.7	200	350	25	123	701	874
Swi	n/a	n/a	34.1	34	33.7	33.7	n/a	99	12.8	18.5	19.4	152	187	199	5.7	5.2	5.3	93	13.5	12.2	12.7	116	81.0	79.2	1.52	0.77	0.56	51	73	309	119	0.1	0.1	0.1	100	100	20	20	698	516
Aus	n/a	n/a	50.3	51	52.3	36.4	n/a	72	23.4	26.4	28.4	121	276	222	6.1	5.4	5.8	95	10.8	11.1	11.4	106	81.9	79.4	0.25	0.58	0.76	232	131	73	165	0.2	0.3	0.5	100	167	36	83	585	712
Fra	39.3	46.6	50.7	51.1	52.9	56	57.0	112	24.9	28.4	31.9	128	278	316	6.3	5.6	5.7	90	11.6	11.5	10.2	87.9	85.7	76.1	0.75	0.75	0.87	66	116	235	186	0.4	0.4	1.4	133	300	52	195	784	1044
Spa	23.6	34.2	43.4	39.1	38.3	45.8	43.3	111	19.7	21.6	26.8	136	221	251	4.6	4.3	4.8	104	10.3	11.1	10.5	102	66.6	68.8	0.62	0.16	0.61	26	381	127	160	0.0	0.4	0.6	400	150	20	98	521	745
Por	n/a	n/a	42.6	46.7	48.3	48.3	n/a	113	12.4	22.5	25.2	203	227	275	5.1	5.3	5.3	104	11.7	11.6	10.7	91.5	73.4	73.5	0.69	0.46	0.50	67	109	145	111	0.0	0.0	0.4	100	0	5	60	529	653
Ita	33.5	41.7	54.4	45.5	47.1	51.9	50.0	110	21.4	24.9	28.6	134	230	282	4.7	4.3	4.3	91	9.0	9.0	8.6	95.6	65.3	61.0	1.03	0.41	0.41	40	100	215	92	0.1	0.2	0.6	200	300	25	05	646	506
Hun	n/a	n/a	47.2	49.6	50.5	50.7	n/a	107	12.9	23.6	22.1	171	242	275	5.2	5.2	4.7	90	12.9	10.4	9.4	72.9	73.0	64.6	0.21	0.19	0.78	73	411	49	197	0.1	0.1	0.6	100	600	20	20	485	641
Cze	n/a	n/a	40.4	41.8	45.9	41.8	n/a	103	14.6	18.8	20.6	141	215	233	4.8	4.2	4.5	94	8.7	9.9	10.4	120	67.4	66.1	0.09	0.18	0.30	600	167	78	77	0.1	0.1	0.4	100	400	20	80	468	602
Pol	n/a	n/a	42.0	44.5	44.4	41.5	n/a	99	14.9	20.0	20.0	138	222	231	5.2	4.9	4.9	94	11.9	11.6	11.4	95.8	73.4	69.9	0.25	0.15	0.22	90	122	31	100	0.2	n/a	0.5	175	250	39	88	478	547
Slo	n/a	n/a	52.0	39.6	41.5	45.6	n/a	88	18.6	15.7	18.4	58.9	264	238	4.3	5.0	4.9	98	14.1	10.5	4.1	29.1	69.0	80.9	0.15	0.18	0.23	147	147	65	59	0.1	0.1	0.3	100	400	20	80	507	619
Ire	n/a	n/a	30.9	33.4	48.9	35.1	n/a	114	17.2	16.3	21.0	122	182	206	5.0	4.9	6.2	124	12.2	13.5	13.1	107	73.8	86.7	1.41	0.51	0.88	36	173	286	193	0.1	0.3	0.5	300	167	30	83	676	738
UK	42.1	45.7	42.2	37.8	42.8	51.6	43.2	114	16.3	20.5	21.7	33	209	241	5.0	5.4	6.0	120	11.4	11.7	12.2	107	72.8	83.6	0.26	0.05	0.06	19	120	54	24	0.4	0.4	1.1	100	275	65	179	539	790
US	32.4	33.8	36.5	33.7	36.5	42.2	38.1	113	13.1	16.2	21.6	65	189	223	4.7	5.3	5.1	109	12.6	14.1	13.6	108	70.5	75.4	0.12	0.12	0.11	100	92	34	31	0.0	0.1	0.4	100	400	5	80	374	565
Aus	n/a	n/a	36.2	34.7	35.3	36.4	n/a	101	13.1	16.0	19.0	45	196	208	4.9	4.3	4.8	98	13.8	13.7	14.4	104	72.8	72.5	0.57	0.18	0.23	132	128	127	59	0.2	0.2	0.6	100	300	45	05	559	422
NZ	n/a	n/a	37.6	37.7	41.9	40.0	n/a	106	21.2	18.4	20.8	98.1	213	222	5.6	5.8	7.4	132	16.5	18.1	21.6	131	85.7	108.8	0.61	0.28	0.28	46	100	126	66	0.0	1.1	100	100	25	20	n/a	560	546
Jap	20.0	30.8	32.1	38.8	36.4	37.1	42.0	108	11.1	18.6	23.1	208	209	246	3.6	3.4	3.8	106	9.5	9.4	9.1	95.8	55.6	57.2	0.10	0.05	0.16	50	320	25	64	0.2	0.2	0.4	100	200	35	70	415	564
SK	n/a	n/a	24.7	29.5	30.5	32.4	n/a	131	2.8	7.5	10.4	371	155	201	n/a	4.2	5.0	n/a	16.3	14.8	16.5	101	69.3	76.4	0.04	0.10	0.29	250	290	33	87	0.0	0.8	110	800	16	60	n/a	359	561
Mex	n/a	n/a	19.5	5.5	24.5	n/a	n/a	126	3.2	7.2	7.9	247	122	149	4.2	4.8	5.2	124	22.2	21.7	20.5	92.3	75.0	83.3	0.02	0.01	n/a	25	50	19	7	0.3	0.0	0.6	0	600	45	90	381	503

G1 Globalization 1 (before mid-2000s) (i*200) + (iii/10) + (iii*200s) (ii*200s) (post mid-2000s) (ii*200s) (ii*200)+(iii/200)+(iii*200).
G2 Globalization 1, G2 Globalization 2

Sources: Elaborated from OECD National Accounts, Social Expenditure data, Family database, Education at a Glance, Employment Outlook

Table A3. Education Equality

Country	1A (a) 1995	1A (b) 2007	1A (c) 2011	1A (d) Trend	1B (a) 1995	1B (b) 2007	1B (c) 2011	1B (d) Trend	1S Score	2 (a) 2001	2 (b) 2007	2 (c) 2013	2 (S) Score	3 (a) 1995	3 (b) 2000	3 (c) 2007	3 (d) 2013	3 (T)	3 (S)	4A (i) 2000	4A (ii) 2007	4A (iii) 2013	4B (i) Public	4B (ii) Private	4 (C)	4 (S) Score	5A(2006) (i)	5A(2006) (ii)	5A(2006) (iii)	5B(2015) (i)	5B(2015) (ii)	5B(2015) (iii)	6 G1	6 G2
Denmark	7.3	7.8	8.7	119	12.2	15.4	15.2	125	114	86	85	82	84	99	98	97	94	95	189	97.8	98.1	97.0	108	135	80	274	11.8	12.6	107	11	11	100	1069	1090
Finland	6.8	6.8	6.8	100	11.0	12.5	12.2	111	91	87	87	90	92	98	97	96	96	98	194	99.3	99.0	99.0	104	75	130	328	9.9	12.5	126	9	9	100	1106	1038
Sweden	7.1	6.7	6.8	96	10.7	12.7	12.3	115	91	91	91	82	87	94	91	89	90	96	186	99.0	100	100	101	74	130	330	12.1	11.4	94	16	12	133	1008	1120
Norway	7.9	6.7	8.7	110	15.5	16.4	14.9	96	112	93	83	81	77	94	96	97	96	102	198	100	100	100	109	100	109	309	10	11	110	10	11	110	1124	1126
Germany	4.6	4.5	5.0	109	8.5	10.3	11.0	129	73	85	85	87	86	89	88	85	86	97	183	87.3	86.3	87.0	105	97	108	282	15.8	13.0	82	13	13	100	861	913
Netherlands	5.1	5.3	5.9	116	9.1	11.7	11.9	131	83	74	83	85	88	79	77	72	70	89	159	85.6	86.7	87.0	109	100	109	283	16.2	16.2	100	16	16	100	896	936
Belgium	5.8	5.9	6.5	112	12.1	12.4	12.2	101	88	83	82	88	86	80	n/a	85	84	105	n/a	94.7	95.2	96.0	104	79	130	322	9.1	9.7	107	9	10	111	912	1037
Switz.	5.7	5.2	5.3	93	13.5	12.2	15.7	116	79	92	90	90	91	72	85	n/a	n/a	n/a	n/a	89.2	86.1	86.0	113	91	124	296	n/a	11.8	n/a	12	n/a	n/a	n/a	n/a
Austria	6.1	5.4	5.8	95	10.8	11.1	11.4	106	79	87	87	90	91	96	96	85	95	95	194	95.8	96.0	96.0	105	100	105	297	10.5	11.8	112	9	10	111	1033	1035
France	6.3	5.6	5.7	90	11.6	11.5	10.2	88	76	78	83	85	87	85	85	84	70	93	163	92.6	92.7	91.0	100	106	94	276	13.9	15.5	112	15	18	120	1011	993
Spain	4.6	4.3	4.8	104	10.3	11.1	10.5	102	69	57	65	66	61	74	74	79	69	93	162	93.0	92.9	88.0	87	164	53	229	11.2	15.0	134	15	14	127	988	962
Portugal	5.1	5.3	5.3	104	11.7	11.6	10.7	91	73	32	44	65	61	97	93	70	58	60	148	99.9	99.9	88.0	106	99	107	283	8.0	8.9	111	10	14	140	978	990
Italy	4.7	4.3	4.3	91	9.0	9.0	8.6	96	61	57	68	84	82	83	76	70	67	81	148	97.8	96.8	96.0	85	121	70	262	10.3	7.3	71	11	12	92	816	858
Hungary	5.2	5.2	4.7	90	12.9	10.4	9.4	73	65	81	85	87	85	80	78	63	79	107	142	n/a	n/a	92.0	76	151	50	234	11.3	11.1	98	11	13	110	952	855
Czech R.	4.8	4.2	4.5	94	8.7	9.9	10.4	120	66	92	94	95	95	72	85	84	99	107	184	90.7	91.7	91.0	105	102	103	285	10.4	10.3	99	12	10	83	897	874
Poland	5.2	4.9	4.9	94	11.9	11.6	11.4	96	70	92	92	94	95	67	67	72	80	119	199	95.4	98.6	92.0	103	136	76	260	12.8	9.2	72	11	10	80	816	890
Slovakia	4.6	3.6	4.6	100	14.1	10.5	18.4	130	76	94	94	92	93	95	95	85	76	80	156	97.6	89.3	89.0	109	86	130	309	14.1	13.2	94	12	12	94	994	974
Ireland	5	4.9	6.2	124	12.2	13.5	13.1	107	87	73	83	90	95	70	79	85	86	123	209	88.7	n/a	95.0	97	193	50	240	14.5	14.6	100	14	14	100	925	1007
UK	5	5.4	6.0	120	11.4	11.7	12.2	107	84	68	75	86	85	80	68	36	57	71	128	91.6	78.1	84.0	134	264	51	209	18.6	7.2	39	15	7	47	736	751
US	4.7	5.3	5.1	109	12.6	14.1	13.6	108	75	88	87	90	88	68	65	50	42	65	135	82.9	91.4	92.0	94	89	106	290	15.7	10.7	68	16	10	63	769	773
Australia	4.9	4.3	4.8	98	13.8	17.7	14.4	104	73	71	81	87	89	65	50	44	35	100	135	n/a	92.0	82.0	119	124	96	260	12.3	11.9	97	13	12	92	894	851
NZ	5.6	5.8	7.4	132	16.5	18.1	21.6	131	109	82	80	81	81	63	66	52	32	82	171	85.6	85.6	83.0	123	126	98	264	17.0	15.9	94	13	13	81	938	958
Japan	3.6	3.4	3.8	106	9.5	9.4	9.1	96	57	94	97	98	99	35	39	33	23	100	135	89.9	89.9	93.0	106	76	130	316	15.2	13.2	87	14	12	86	773	779
S. Korea	n/a	4.2	5.0	119	16.3	14.8	16.5	101	78	95	97	98	98	n/a	23	21	32	139	171	80.8	77.8	84.0	118	76	130	299	20.8	20.8	100	15	17	113	850	934
Mexico	4.2	4.8	5.2	124	22.2	21.7	20.5	92	83	25	39	46	50	77	79	71	68	88	156	86.1	82.1	83.0	118	120	98	264	35.8	23.8	66	37	18	49	855	804

Column headings:

- **Column 1A:** Public expenditure on education in GDP, (a) 1995, (b) 2007, (c) 2011, (d) Trend to 2011, 1995 as 100
- **Column 1B:** Public expenditure on education in public spending, (a) 1995, (b) 2007, (c) 2011, (d) Trend to 2011, 1995 as 100
- **Column 1S:** Score = (Aa*10) + (Ad/20) + (Bc)+ (Bd/20)
- **Column 2:** % Population with upper secondary education (25-34 y/o), (a) 2001, (b) 2007, (c) 2013, (S) Score = a+c/2+((b-a (to max 15))
- **Column 3:** Share of public spending on tertiary educational institutions, (a) 1995, (b) 2000, (c) 2007, (d) 2013, (T) Trend = 95 as 100, (S) Score = T+d
- **Column 4:** Public/private education spending in GDP (primary, secondary & post-secondary non-tertiary), (C) = (B/Bi)*100 (to maximum of 130), (S) Score = (Aiii*2)+C. (A) Public: (i) 2000, (ii) 2007, (iii) 2013. (B) 2008 as 100: (i) Public, (ii) Private.
- **Column 5:** Ratio of students to teaching staff, secondary (i) state, (ii) private, (iii) it as % of1. (A) 2006, (B) 2015, % of1.
- **Column 6:** (S) Score = (1B*10)+(2)+(3*2)+(4*2)+(5iii*3)***

*** Column 6 Score: G1: (1Aa*20) + (1Ba*10) + 2a + (3a*2) + (4Ai*2) + (5Aiii *3), G2: (1Ac*20) + (1Bc*10) + 2c + (3d*2) + (4Aiii*2) + (5Biii*3),

Sources: Elaborated from OECD Education at a Glance

Table A4a. Relative Employment and Income Returns to Education, Females

Column legend:
- **Column 1:** (A) Public spending on GDP, (B) Public spending on education in public spending, (a) 2000, (b) 2007, (c) 2015
- **Column 2:** % Population with upper secondary education (age 25–34); (i) 2000, (ii) 2007, (iii) 2014
- **Column 3:** Share of public spending on tertiary educational institutions; (i) 2000, (ii) 2007, (iii) 2014
- **Column 4:** Public/private education spending in GDP (primary, secondary and post-secondary non-tertiary), (i) 2000, (ii) 2007, (iii) 2014, (A) Public, (B) Private
- **Column 5:** Education employment return rate, females (a) 2002, (b) 2008, (c) 2014, (i) lower secondary, (ii) as % of tertiary, to max of 80
- **Column 6:** Education unemployment return rate, females (a) 2002, (b) 2008, (c) 2014, (i) lower secondary, (ii) as % of tertiary, to max of 80

Country	C1 A(a)	A(b)	A(c)	C1 B(a)	B(b)	B(c)	C2 (i)	(ii)	(iii)	C3 (i)	(ii)	(iii)	C4 Pub(i)	(ii)	(iii)	Priv(i)	(ii)	(iii)	C5 (ai)	(aii)	(bi)	(bii)	(ci)	(cii)	C6 (ai)	(aii)	(bi)	(bii)	(ci)	(cii)
Denmark	8.3	7.8	8.6	15.3	15.4	15.2	86	85	82	98	97	95	98	98	97	2.2	1.9	2.8	52	62	60	58	58	66	4.6	100	3.4	65	8.3	55
Finland	6.0	5.9	7.2	12.5	12.5	12.3	87	90	90	97	96	96	99	99	99	0.7	1.0	0.7	54	64	61	55	54	63	8.1	38	9.8	38	13.2	34
Sweden	7.2	6.7	7.7	13.4	12.7	14.9	91	91	82	89	89	89	100	100	100	0.1	0.1	1.0	69	78	65	72	68	75	3.9	54	6.9	42	14.5	26
Norway	5.9	6.7	7.4	14.5	16.4	17.0	93	83	81	96	97	96	99	100	100	1.0	1.0	1.0	57	61	63	80	60	66	2.1	81	4.5	33	5.9	36
Germany	4.4	4.5	5.0	9.8	10.3	11.1	85	85	87	88	85	86	86	87	87	13.7	13.5	12.1	45	56	51	63	57	66	6.4	59	13.5	30	10.0	27
Netherlands	5.0	5.3	5.5	11.2	12.0	12.0	74	83	85	77	72	70	86	87	88	14.3	13.3	13.4	50	61	55	64	53	60	2.2	91	4.0	37	10.4	39
Belgium	5.9	5.9	6.6	12.1	12.4	12.0	75	82	82	92	90	88	95	96	96	5.3	4.8	3.8	45	55	57	57	44	51	6.0	65	11.4	32	13.8	30
Switzerland	5.4	5.2	5.1	15.6	12.2	15.5	92	90	91	n/a	n/a	n/a	89	86	86	10.8	13.9	11.7	62	76	62	74	69	79	2.7	100	8.4	34	8.8	39
Austria	5.6	5.4	5.5	10.7	11.1	10.5	83	87	90	96	85	94	n/a	95	95	4.2	4.0	4.1	48	56	50	61	54	62	2.9	83	6.9	32	8.9	43
France	6.0	5.6	5.5	11.6	11.5	9.7	78	83	85	84	85	79	93	91	91	7.4	7.3	8.2	56	70	58	73	55	64	9.4	5	10.6	42	13.7	37
Spain	4.3	4.3	4.3	10.9	11.1	9.6	57	65	66	74	79	68	88	93	88	7.0	7.1	8.9	44	58	52	61	61	70	10.1	83	15.7	39	33.3	46
Portugal	5.4	5.3	5.1	12.6	11.6	9.9	32	44	65	93	70	62	100	100	100	0.1	0.1	0.1	77	80	73	80	66	74	5.0	96	11.0	62	16.6	68
Italy	4.5	4.5	4.1	9.8	9.0	8.0	57	68	74	78	70	65	97	94	94	2.2	2.3	3.8	39	42	56	41	41	51	6.1	97	12.7	42	6.3	65
Hungary	4.9	5.2	4.7	13.9	14.3	9.4	81	85	87	70	70	70	+95	+95	+95	8.3	8.0	8.0	35	45	46	58	46	58	3.1	48	15.3	16	17.1	17
Czech Republic	4.0	4.2	4.1	9.5	9.9	9.6	92	94	95	85	84	76	92	91	91	8.3	9.3	9.1	42	53	42	54	47	59	8.6	19	17.3	9	20.3	15
Poland	5.0	4.9	4.9	12.7	11.6	11.6	52	92	94	67	72	81	99	99	92	1.4	4.6	6.1	32	39	30	32	36	41	11.2	54	11.9	29	17.8	26
Slovak Republic	3.9	3.6	4.2	14.7	10.5	10.2	52	94	94	74	76	77	98	89	89	2.4	11.4	10.7	33	36	37	37	45	57	16.0	19	34.8	10	34.7	20
Ireland	4.3	4.9	5.3	13.6	13.5	13.5	73	83	90	79	85	74	96	95	95	5.2	5.2	5.2	47	56	48	58	37	45	2.5	44	5.3	4	14.8	38
United Kingdom	4.3	5.4	5.7	11.0	13.9	13.9	68	75	86	68	36	28	89	81	81	11.3	14.3	16.4	48	50	48	55	55	66	6.8	38	8.2	22	7.4	35
United States	4.9	5.3	5.4	14.4	14.1	14.5	88	87	90	31	32	35	92	91	91	8.4	8.6	8.4	49	61	58	55	48	61	5.5	38	9.7	22	12.7	29
Australia	4.5	4.3	5.2	13.8	13.8	14.5	71	81	87	50	44	39	83	81	86	17.1	16.4	11.2	51	63	58	58	56	69	3.4	59	5.2	35	8.2	40
New Zealand	6.8	5.8	6.4	14.5	18.1	18.0	82	80	81	n/a	66	51	n/a	83	n/a	n/a	11.2	7.0	54	57	72	72	68	79	3.0	80	4.1	56	5.2	64
Japan	3.6	3.4	3.6	9.5	9.4	9.3	94	n/a	n/a	23	33	34	90	92	87	10.2	10.1	7.0	53	n/a	56	n/a	n/a	n/a	2.6	100	1.6	80	4.0	75
South Korea	3.7	4.2	5.1	16.3	16.3	19.1	95	97	98	21	21	34	81	78	82	19.2	22.2	19.3	60	58	58	60	60	80	1.0	100	1.6	100	1.9	100
Mexico	4.4	4.8	5.3	23.4	21.7	19.1	25	39	46	79	71	71	86	82	82	13.9	17.9	17.4	48	80	67	80	45	61	0.5	20	2.7	20	3.2	100

Share of public spending in tertiary education in 2000 OECD Education at a glance 2003, Table B3.2: India 18.3. Uruguay 99.7. Indonesia 43.8. Argentina 66.2 Philippines 34.4. Paraguay 62.6. Thailand 80.4. in 2014, in Chile public in tertiary was 36, and in prim-post-secon. non-tertiary, it was 83.

The figures for Hungary for Column 3 (i and ii) and Hungary and Ireland Column 4 (Ai and ii) are proxies, based on repeating the figure for 2014, as earlier data not available

Sources: Elaborated from OECD Education at a Glance

Table A4b. Relative Employment and Income Returns to Education, Females

Column 7: Relative Education Income Return Rates, Females (upper secondary/post-secondary nontertiary as 100), (a) 1999/00, (b) 2007, (c) 2015*, (i) lower secondary, (ii) tertiary, (iii) lower secondary as % of tertiary

Column 8: (A) 70–X, where X = Female Long-Term Unemployment Rate (as % of total), (B) Unemployment Rate Both Genders, (S) Score = A+B (20b–y²2)

Column 9: Earning Dispersion 9th–1st Earning Deciles (i) 1998, (ii) 2014, (S) Score = (5–5ii)*50

Column 10: Returns to Equal Education Scores (E) Education*, (R) Returns*=, (i) 98/02, (ii) 2014 (or latest)

Column 11: Trade union density 1980 (i), 2013 (ii)

	C7 (ai)	(aii)	(aiii)	(bi)	(bii)	(biii)	(ci)	(cii)	(ciii)	C8 (A)2000	(A)2008	(A)2015	(B)2000	(B)2008	(B)2015	(S)2000	(S)2008	(S)2015	C9 (i)	(ii)	C10 (E)i	(E)ii	(R)i	(R)ii	C11 1980	2013
Den	90	123	73	83	124	67	81	128	63	50	57.3	43.8	4.3	3.5	6.2		81	90	2.48	2.56	435	431	730	702	78.6	66.8
Fin	99	145	68	96	146	66	98	142	70	44	53.8	49.0	8.4	6.4	9.4	64	82	80	2.42	2.57	412	423	603	593	69.4	69.0
Swe	88	126	70	84	127	66	87	125	70	47	58.7	54.5	5.6	6.2	7.4	76	78	87	2.24	2.28	422	422	704	641	78.0	67.7
Nor	83	135	61	81	134	60	77	134	57	67	64.0	59.9	3.2	2.5	4.4	101	97		1.95	2.42	412	428	658	561	58.3	52.1
Ger	72	137	53	84	159	53	72	159	45	19	19.0	28.4	7.4	7.4	4.6	44	48	50	3.07	3.41	356	365	533	466	35.3	18.1
NL	72	155	46	75	159	47	76	158	48	30	37.8	29.0	3.7	3.7	6.9	64	64	72	2.88	2.94	347	356	662	513	34.8	17.8
Bel	82	132	62	81	134	60	81	151	54	13	21.9	19.3	8.4	7	8.5	39	48	63	2.39	2.46	391	399	594	485	54.1	55.1
Swi	72	144	50	76	156	49	73	153	48	40	30.1	29.2	2.6	3.5	4.5	75	75	68	2.53	2.48	n/a	n/a	598	542	27.7	16.2
Aus	74	156	47	73	160	46	78	151	48	47	47.4	44.1	5.6	4.1	5.7	80	79	79	3.26	3.33	396	395	530	524	56.7	27.8
Fra	79	145	54	82	147	56	77	153	50	27	33.5	26.5	8.9	7.4	10.4	49	37	53	3.05	2.98	381	368	532	531	18.3	7.7
Spa	64	125	51	70	149	47	70	174	40	18	41.1	17.2	11.3	11.3	22.1	37	58	61	3.10	3.12	341	330	435	440	8.3	16.9
Por	63	170	37	67	173	39	72	171	42	30	24.9	14.0	4.4	8.8	12.7	62	50	49	4.31	3.89	376	331	539	469	54.8	18.9
Ita	84	137	61	74	143	52	71	135	53	9	22.5	11.2	10.4	6.7	11.9	25	49	48	2.04	2.17	356	339	544	486	49.6	37.3
Hun	71	164	43	71	185	38	73	181	40	24	23.7	24.9	6.3	7.8	6.8	51	51	57	4.21	3.67	364	360	388	431	49.1	10.5
Cze	72	170	42	74	165	45	76	156	49	20	19.9	22.1	8.8	4.4	5.1	43	51	51	2.9	3.52	365	356	388	381	46.3	12.7
Pol	76	148	51	76	165	46	77	158	49	29	39.2	31.2	16.1	7.9	7.5	37	37	43	4.03	4.11	356	373	416	358	54.8	12.7
Slo	n/a	n/a	n/a	71	172	41	70	167	42	15	9.3	31.2	16.4	9.6	11.5	37	25	283,40		3.56	371	353	+399	307	64.2	13.3
Ire	65	163	40	67	178	38	74	164	45	22	50.7	22.5	4.3	6.4	9.4	54	78	63	3.93	3.96	364	376	499	428	54.3	29.6
UK	69	176	39	70	181	39	71	169	46	51	51.9	22.5	4.8	5.6	5.3	80	81	80	3.47	3.56	334	316	443	++437	49.7	25.8
US	62	164	38	61	167	37	61	177	34	65	59.7	52.8	5.1	5.8	5.3	97	88	88	4.51	5.01	322	331	412	348	22.1	10.8
Aus	89	146	61	86	146	59	94	163	58	46	56.0	48.3	5	4.2	6.1	73	73	84	2.91	3.47	310	310	546	490	47.7	17.0
NZ	86	126	67	85	126	67	85	139	61	56	66.6	57.5	3.8	4.2	5.8	84	99	95	2.64	2.95	362	340	610	582	31.1	19.8
Jap	78	161	48	n/a	n/a		72	116	62	53	46.2	49.8	4.4	4	3.4	84	78	85	2.98	2.94	307	340	488	+482	31.1	17.8
Sk	69	141	49	97	167	58	80	150	53	69	69.6	69.7	3.7	3.2	3.6	100	100	106	3.83	4.79	286	300[7]	587	564	14.7	10.1
Mex	n/a	n/a	n/a	47	187	25	55	195	28	68	68.2	68.7	3	4	4.4	103	103	106	2.75	3.88	330	330	=443	428	24.3	13.6

*For 2015 Bachelors or equivalent. Sweden, Spain, Japan and S. Korea are total tertiary. Red are 2005 figures. Column 7: In Denmark the greater difference in earnings is between bachelors and masters +115–162, compared with 165 to 205 in the UK. Whereas there is less difference in Denmark between secondary and bachelors at 81–115, compared with 77–169 in the UK. The UK mirrors the pattern of highly unequal less developed countries, where the greatest difference is also between secondary and bachelors, for example 67–268 in Chile, and –in the same country a lesser distance between bachelors and masters plus of 268–440. Blue is 2010. Red is 2005. Green is 2012. + The Slovak Republic Figure uses the 2000 data. ++ The UK figure for Column 7.++ The UK figure for Column 5, Table A.3 uses the 2007 figure. The Japanese figure for column 5 uses the 2007 figure. —=Column 7 for Mexico Ri score relies on 2007 in place of 2000 data.

Sources: Elaborated from OECD Education at a Glance, Employment Outlook

Table A5. Structure of Employment and Non-Employment Time

	Column 1: Average annual leisure hours		Column 2: Share of part-time employment		Column 3: Share of part-time employment males		Column 4: Share of part-time employment females		Column 5:			Column 6: Parental leave and child-care quality**2014/5				Column 7:		Column 8:		Column 9:				Column 10:		Column 11:	
	2000	2015/6	2009	2015	2009	2015	2009	2015/6	(ii)	(iii)	(S)	(i)	(ii)	(iii)	(S)	2014	(S)	2014	(S)	(i)	(iii)	(iv)	(S)	2012	(S)	(S)	(SG)
Den	1534	1590	18.9	20.0	13.6	15.0	24.8	25.8	45	58	129	27.0	1.1	6	82	13	87	57	243	20.2	23.1	6.2	30.0	11.9	88.1	466	170
Fin	1258	1347	12.2	13.4	8.7	10.6	15.9	16.4	54	65	120	42.6	6.4	10	90	18	82	76	224	21.0	24.9	9.4	32.1	23.1	76.9	467	162
Swe	1358	1379	14.6	14.1	10.0	10.6	19.8	18.0	44	59	134	38.1	7.6	5	107	16	84	53	247	21.1	32.4	7.4	31.6	5.8	94.2	508	178
Nor	1545	1576	20.4	20.4	11.3	11.3	30.4	27.6	32	44	138	45.5	9.9	5	116	28	72	49	251	20.7	38.3	4.4	31.0	14.9	85.1	490	154
Ger	1547	1637	21.9	22.4	9.3	9.3	38.1	37.4	19	25	132	42.6	5.7	7	86	9	91	105	195	21.2	6.0	4.6	31.6	11.2	88.8	375	137
NL	1538	1570	36.7	38.5	17.0	19.5	59.9	60.7	28	32	114	16.0	0.4	7	84	45	55	121	179	20.7	6.4	6.9	31.6	23.5	76.5	365	131
Bel	1405	1449	18.3	18.2	6.6	7.3	31.8	30.2	18	24	133	15.0	5.0	14	67	14	86	94	206	21.1	-1.7	8.5	32.7	11.2	88.8	344	129
Aus	1326	1410	19.0	21.0	6.7	8.6	32.2	35.0	19	24	126	7.9	9.0	16	44	26	74	134	166	20.1	11.4	4.2	29.6	28.0	72.0	n/a	108
Swi	1193	1399	26.5	26.8	9.2	10.9	46.7	45.0	19	24	124	51.2	5.9	9	97	41	59	90	210	20.8	5.7	6.5	32.5	3.4	96.6	383	139
Fra	1465	1528	13.3	14.5	5.1	6.9	22.5	22.3	22	31	141	18.8	5.7	15	67	34	66	104	196	20.6	5.7	9.7	33.7	13.1	86.9	365	133
Spa	1247	1305	11.9	14.5	4.4	7.2	21.4	23.1	18	31	172	38.1	2.1	15	61	34	66	104	196	20.3	-1.5	22.1	34.5	7.9	92.1	374	139
Por	1083	1158	9.6	10.5	5.9	8.5	13.8	12.6	20	68	340	20.0	11.5	17	79	20	80	232	68	21.5	-7.4	12.5	32.7	5.8	94.2	412	175
Ita	1149	1270	15.8	18.7	5.5	8.0	30.5	32.2	18	26	144	25.2	0.2	13	58	44	56	211	89	21.3	-8.9	12.0	33.4	5.7	94.3	296	137
Hun	1155	1239	3.6	4.4	2.3	3.0	6.2	7.4	36	50	139	71.1	1.0	13	72	16	84	141	159	18.5	3.3	6.8	29.0	5.1	94.9	394	162
Cze	1104	1230	3.8	4.7	2.1	2.5	6.2	7.4	29	34	117	56.3	0.0	13	66	44	56	141	159	18.3	1.7	5.1	28.9	18.0	82.0	n/a	133
Pol	1012	1070	8.7	6.4	5.0	3.8	13.1	9.6	40	40	100	20.0	2.0	16	53	24	76	139	161	20.9	10.7	7.5	32.6	6.9	93.1	358	147
Slo	1184	1260	3.0	5.7	2.2	4.1	4.1	7.8	32	53	166	52.5	0.0	10	73	65	35	n/a	133	18.1	-12.3	11.5	28.4	28.0	72.0	n/a	145
Ire	1067	1121	23.7	23.3	10.9	12.3	37.4	25.4	44	50	159	9.1	0.0	14	50	56	44	167	133	20.0	-7.6	9.8	31.8	41.6	58.4	285	109
UK	1300	1324	23.9	24.0	10.9	11.9	38.8	37.7	25	32	128	12.2	6.4	10	64	72	28	117	183	9.0	19.3	5.6	28.6	45.0	55.0	326	107
US	1166	1217	14.7	12.7	9.2	8.4	19.2	17.4	44	48	109	0.0	0.0	12	54	37	63	93	207	21.0	31.3	3.1	24.6	39.7	60.3	382	126
Aus	1221	1331	24.7	25.2	13.2	14.2	38.1	36.0	39	37	94.9	7.6	0.8	5	79	37	63	139	161	9.9	26.5	6.1	20.4	20.9	79.1	371	141
NZ	1166	1217	22.5	21.3	11.9	11.2	34.4	32.7	29	34	117	7.6	0.0	7	71	28	72	123	177	26.5	36.8	5.8	35.3	40.4	59.6	372	117
Jap	1179	1207	20.3	22.7	10.5	12.0	33.8	35.9	31	33	106	35.8	30.4	14	71	38	62	237	63	44.5	14.5	3.4	54.9	21.7	78.3	426	127
SK	488	931	9.9	10.6	6.9	8.5	14.2	15.9	51	44	86.3	25.3	16.1	9	118	34	66	182	118	18.1	49.6	3.6	96.5	13.0	87.0	447	152
Mex	689	745	17.9	18.2	12.0	12.5	27.8	27.5	38	45	118	12.0	1.0	15	21	38	62	260	40	31.9	48.8	4.3	110.7	33.3	66.6	321	117

Column 5: Mates' part-time share as % of females' share ( ) 2006, (ii) 2015, (iii) Trend to ** ; i as 100. (iii) 2015, (S) Score = 300-X.

Column 7: Difference in female/male time for care work. Eally minutes, over 15s, (S) Score = 100-X.

Column 8: Difference in female/male time for unpaid care work (in minutes per day), (S) Score = 300-X.

Column 9: Employment security (2015), (i) % of employment 10 years+, (ii) 50% of unemployment 1 year <, (iii) Unemployment, (iv) 55-59 age group with <5 years job tenure, (S) Score = (i)+(ii)+(30-iii)+(iv/10).

Column 10: Net costs child-care fees, (S) Score = 100-X

Column 11: Final score (S) = (1/10)+(1/10)+(5ii+2+5iii/3)+(9)+(10)+(Score of Table A6/50). Score for gendered structure of public child care (SG) = (5ii)+(30+30-6iii)+(10)

Table A6a. Structure of Control of Core Human Activities, Social Relations, and Forms of Time – OECD countries

Column 1: Annual leisure hours, (3000 - average annual employment hours)
Column 2: Male part-time share as % of female share
Column 3: Paid maternity and parental leave, full-rate, equivalent weeks
Column 4.1: Task and time controls, (A) 2005, (B) 2010, (a) low-skilled manual, (b) Total, (i) Able to choose/change order of tasks, (ii) Some control of work-time (working time not set by employer), (iii) Work gives feeling of work well done
Column 4.2: Task and time controls, (A) 2005, (B) 2010, (i) Able to choose/change order of tasks, (ii) Some control of work-time (working time not set by employer), (iii) Work gives feeling of work well done. Equality of control and well-being across skill levels. Low-skilled manual as a percentage of total (to a maximum of 100%).
4.3: Total equality score
4.4 iv 2005-2010 Overall equality difference

	Col 1 a 2000	Col 1 b 2010	Col 1 c 2015	Col 2 2000	Col 2 2009	Col 2 2015	Col 3 a 98-02	Col 3 b 2008	Col 3 c 2015	4.1 (i) Tasks (A)a	(A)b	(B)a	(B)b	4.1 (ii) Time (A)a	(A)b	(B)a	(B)b	4.1 (iii) Well-being (A)a	(A)b	(B)a	(B)b	4.2 Tasks 2015	2010	4.2 Time 2015	2010	4.2 Well-being 2005	2010	4.3 1 2005	4.3 2 2010	4.4 iv
Den	1534	1458	1590	39	45	58	24.0	32.2	27.07	85	74	74	43	59	46	59	59	88	90	88	91	91	100	73	78	98	97	262	275	+13
Fin	1258	1303	1347	51	54	65	12.0	35.7	42.67	89	85	70	31	54	55	31	54	70	72	74	74	77	93	65	57	87	97	229	247	+18
Swe	1358	1376	1379	34	44	59	14.4	37.7	38.17	85	91	61	48	55	66	54	62	84	78	82	78	89	83	64	77	87	97	240	257	+17
Nor	1545	1586	1576	26	32	44	42.0	38.8	45.56	65	78	81	25	42	66	48	53	87	89	87	89	83	70	53	53	102	102	238	223	-15
Ger	1547	1581	1637	14	19	25	14.0	54.6	42.63	57	82	58	34	28	43	34	45	78	80	84	86	63	68	65	73	74	93	202	234	+32
NL	1538	1623	1570	23	28	32	16.0	21.3	16.06	52	39	50	43	50	63	43	65	71	86	90	84	76	80	79	66	83	93	238	239	+01
Bel	1405	1449	1449	21	18	24	11.0	14.4	15.05	79	64	71	27	22	47	27	45	83	83	86	86	73	79	47	64	83	97	208	240	+32
Swi	1326	1360	1410	19	19	24	16.0	12.8	7.9	na	na	na	na	na	na	na	na	na	na	na	na	73	79	47	64	88	97			
Aus	1193	1413	1399	11	17	21	16.0	35.3	51.24	65	69	47	35	35	52	30	47	95	76	91	88	66	68	64	64	125	91	234	235	+01
Fra	1465	1449	1528	22	22	31	18.0	43.8	18.85	62	68	69	46	29	46	81	39	83	87	82	84	72	72	63	208	95	91	232	270	+38
Spa	1247	1337	1305	16	18	31	16.0	16.0	16.05	40	54	54	28	33	28	20	87	68	73	77	83	125	86	85	23	93	93	278	202	-76
Por	1083	1286	1158	33	20	68	6.0	17.0	20.04	58	55	55	22	16	25	22	25	81	77	85	77	76	87	64	88	93	86	238	266	+28
Ita	1149	1222	1270	24	18	26	16.0	23.8	25.23	60	71	44	25	25	51	51	41	84	87	84	87	65	103	59	80	101	85	221	277	+56
Hun	1155	1039	1239	33	36	50	17.0	76.1	71.15	56	63	64	28	21	28	11	28	75	67	78	78	89	90	75	39	103	86	264	215	-49
Cze	1104	1053	1230	30	29	34	19.0	63.4	56.34	63	36	55	30	37	32	30	40	77	67	79	79	71	65	86	75	95	103	257	225	-32
Pol	1012	1061	1070	49	40	40	16.0	39.1	41.64	42	47	64	38	29	38	55	22	81	77	77	77	75	73	76	76	95	91	246	264	+18
Slo	1184	1214	1260	35	32	53	15.4	46.1	52.5	na	na	na	na	na	na	na	na	na	na	na	na	80	58	68	250	88	88			
Ire	1067	1336	1121	24	22	35	12.6	6.6	9.15	71	39	39	47	47	32	47	25	82	72	82	72	76	74	72	58	88	88	236	204	-32
UK	1300	1353	1324	21	25	32	5.4	12.8	12.25	52	70	70	25	34	47	25	42	68	74	59	75	76	74	72	59	92	79	240	212	-28

Sources: Elaborated from OECD Employment Outlook, Fifth European Survey of Working Conditions, OECD Family Database

Table A6b. Structure of Control of Core Human Activities, Social Relations, and Forms of Time – OECD countries

Column 5: Employment security, (i) % of employment 10 years+, (ii) 50% of unemployment > 1 year (if over 50, score = 0, (iii) Unemployment, (iv) Population with more than 5 years job tenure, age 55-59, (S) Score = i+ii+(30-iii)+(iv/10)

Column 6: Net costs of childcare, (i) 2004/2005, (ii) 2008, (iii) 2012, (S) Score = (100-x)

Column 7: Overall score: (A) (1/50)+(2*2)+(3)+(4.1iay)+(4.1iib)+(4.1iia)+(4.1iiia)+(4.1iiib)+(5*2)+(6*2), (B) A + 4.3 (C) A+ Employment returns score Table A1 + School equality score Table A4 (D) B + Employment returns (Table A4) (E) CPF Table A4

	Col 5 – 2000					Col 5 – 2009					Col 5 – 2015					Col 6			Col 7 (A)		(B)		(C)		(D)		(E)
	i	ii	iii	iv	(S)	i	ii	iii	iv	(S)	i	ii	iii	iv	(S)	i	ii	(S)	00s	10s''	00s	10s	00s	10s	00s	13s	10s
Den	28.5	26.6	4.8	77.9	88.1	25.3	40.5	6.0	65.5	116	25.1	27.5	6.0	84.2	105	92	89	88	935	993	1197	1268	1665	1695	1970	1666	1773
Fin	38.2	25.2	8.4	85.7	114	37.5	33.4	8.2	83.0	121	36.1	23.4	9.0	81.9	110	91	88	77	930	981	1159	1228	1533	1608	1762	1821	1607
Swe	39.2	21.1	7.6	82.9	112	35.5	37.2	8.3	82.1	123	31.6	33.2	6.6	77.9	91	92	93	94	951	967	1191	1238	1655	1643	1895	1879	1651
Nor	31.4	35.5	4.5	83.3	121	32.2	42.3	3.1	68.0	128	31.7	37.5	4.7	45	122	90	83	85	938	976	1176	1199	1596	1537	1834	1760	1465
Ger	40.8	0.0	10.8	84.6	88	41.2	4.5	7.5	83.5	97	40.8	8.8	4.2	82.5	104	91	86	89	723	853	925	1087	1256	1319	1458	1553	1504
NL	37.3	7.0	5.3	85.0	97.5	38.9	25.2	3.4	87.2	119	37.7	7.3	6.1	97.4	103	86	87	86	869	915	1107	1154	1531	1428	1769	1667	1268
Bel	44.0	0.0	8.5	90.2	94.5	42.2	5.8	7.9	89.9	97.1	43.5	0.0	8.5	94.0	48	95	94	90	811	738	1019	978	1405	1223	1613	1474	1262
Swi	3.0	10.9	4.2	82.7	68.0	29.9	19.9	4.4	82.3	104	29.3	13.3	4.4	95.3	67	61	22	72	n/a	n/a	n/a	n/a	n/a	n/a	n/a	n/a	1460
Aus	40.9	24.7	5.2	86.6	120	37.7	28.7	4.8	86.8	120	40.9	20.8	6.2	84.2	110	81	87	87	830	907	1064	1142	1360	1431	1594	1317	n/a
Fra	42.7	8.1	9.2	89.0	120	41.7	14.9	9.5	85.5	106	46.1	5.6	9.9	85.5	85.5	83	83	87	833	889	1065	1121	1365	1420	1597	1478	1280
Spa	33.2	0.5	9.2	82.8	82.8	33.0	26.2	18.0	82.6	99.5	42.5	1.6	19.9	83.7	82.6	70	92	92	671	837	949	1039	1106	1277	1384	1181	1341
Por	39.0	0.0	7.7	87.6	90.1	41.2	5.8	9.6	84.6	95.9	47.3	0.0	11.2	83.7	94.2	93	92	94	767	882	1005	1148	1306	1351	1544	1188	1156
Ita	46.3	0.4	7.7	87.8	97.8	43.3	5.4	7.8	89.1	99.8	49.5	0.0	11.6	88.2	96.7	93	94	94	822	836	1043	1113	1366	1322	1587	1599	1044
Hun	33.4	3.9	7.2	82.7	88.4	32.9	7.6	10.0	80.3	88.5	33.7	2.7	5.2	88.5	88.5	92	94	95	784	855	1048	1070	1172	1286	1436	1333	1185
Cze	32.6	6.3	7.9	82.4	89.2	37.0	18.8	6.7	80.8	108	41.8	6.8	4.1	84.2	103	90	89	92	781	846	1038	1061	1169	1227	1429	1114	1302
Pol	38.7	0.0	8.2	84.1	79.3	34.0	8.2	8.8	76.5	108	36.9	15.0	6.2	82.6	104	85	93	83	824	867	1070	1131	1240	1225	1486	1135	1143
Slo	36.7	26.9	16.3	78.2	105	36.5	6.0	12.0	82.3	82.7	37.6	0.0	9.8	81.0	85.9	89	93	72	n/a	n/a	n/a	n/a	n/a	n/a	n/a	1132	1166
Ire	29.5	18.4	4.4	77.9	101	28.6	20.9	11.9	82.6	79.2	37.1	0.0	7.8	84.5	87.8	55	55	58	755	713	991	917	1254	1141	1490	1176	1068
UK	29.1	17.7	4.8	71.6	99.2	28.1	25.5	7.6	75.3		30.9	25.5	4.9	75.0	109	59	59	55	725	754	965	966	1168	1191	1408	1135	1209

Column 7: (A), (B), (C): 2000s, 2010s latest; (A 10s uses 2015 from column 5; 00s uses 2000, except columns 4 and 6 that uses 2004/5), UK Column 7B, uses the employment return from 2002 as later data not available

Sources: Elaborated from OECD Employment Outlook, OECD Family Database

Notes

Chapter 1: Basic Income in Time

1 Spence, T., 1982 [1775], 'The Real Rights of Man', in T.H. Dickinson (ed.), *The Political Works of Thomas Spence*, Newcastle-upon-Tyne: Avero.

2 Paine, T., 2015 [1795], *Agrarian Justice*, CreateSpace Independent Publishing Platform, p. 26.

3 Friedman, M., 1962, *Capitalism and Freedom*, Chicago, IL: University of Chicago Press, pp. 192–3.

4 https://www.parliament.uk/business/committees/committees-a-z/commons-select/work-and-pensions-committee/news-parliament-2015/citizens-income-report-published-16-17/

5 Bremmer, I. 2012, *Every Nation for Itself*, New York: Portfolio.

6 Barry, B., 2005, *Why Social Justice Matters*, Cambridge: Polity, 68–9, 212.

7 Haagh, L., 2011, 'Working Life, Well-Being and Welfare Reform', *World Development*, 39 (3), 450–73.

8 Germanic and Nordic languages have two words for independence, which translate roughly as autonomous and self-assured (in Danish, 'uafhængig' and 'selvstændig').

9 https://www.theguardian.com/education/2018/apr/02/teachers-warn-of-growing-poverty-crisis-in-british-schools?

10 Karanikolos, M., Heino, P., McKee, M., Stuckler, D. and Legido-Quigley, H., 2016, 'Effects of the Global Financial Crisis on Health in High-Income Countries', *International Journal of Health Services*, 46 (2), 208–40.

11 Barr, B., Taylor-Robinson, D., Stuckler, D., Loopstra, R., Reeves, A. and Whitehead, M., 2016, 'First, Do No Harm: Are Disability Assessments Associated with Adverse Trends in Mental Health? A Longitudinal Ecological Study', *Journal of Epidemiology and Community Health*, 70 (4), 339–45, p. 341.

12 Haagh, L., 2018, 'The Developmental Social Contract and Basic Income in Denmark', *Social Policy and Society*, https://doi.org/10.1017/S1474746418000301.

13 British Medical Association, 2016, 'Health in All Policies', available at https://www.bma.org.uk/collective-voice/policy-and-research/public-and-population-health/health-inequalities

14 Marmot, M., Allen, J., et al., 2010, *Fair Society, Healthy Lives: Strategic Review of Health Inequalities England post 2010*, London: Institute of Health Equity, p. 134.

15 Ibid., p. 91.

16 Pedersen expressed this view in an interview on 2 August 2018: https://www.mm.dk/artikel/ove-k-pedersen - konkurrencestaten - skal - reformeres. See further Campbell, J. and Pedersen O., 2007, 'Institutional Competitiveness in the Global Economy', *Regulation & Governance*, 1 (3), 230–46; and Neilson, D. and Stubbs, T.H., 2016, 'Competition States in the Neo-liberal Era', *Competition & Change*, 20 (2), 122–44.

17 https://leftfootforward.org/2018/02/the-uk-is-mired-in-222bn-of-pfi-debt-heres-how-we-can-take-on-the-public-finance-fat-cats/

18 https://www.socialeurope.eu/reshaping-fiscal-policies-in-europe-enforcing-austerity-attacking-democracy

19 Titmuss, R.M., 1968, *Commitment to Welfare*, London: Allen & Unwin, p. 134.

20 Titmuss, R.M., 1962, *Income Distribution and Social Change*, London: Allen and Unwin, p. 198.

21 Hayek supported 'the certainty of a given minimum of sustenance for all', but not 'the security of a given standard of life'. Von Hayek, F., *The Road to Serfdom*, 1944, London: Routledge Classics, p. 124.

22 Murray, C., 2006, *In Our Hands: A Plan to Replace the Welfare State*, Washington, DC: AEI Press.

23 Zuckerberg, M., 2017, Facebook entry, 5 July.

24 Russell, B., 1935, *In Praise of Idleness and Other Essays*, London: Routledge, pp. 90–2.

25 A good summary is Offe, C., 2009, 'Basic Income and the Labour Contract', *Analyse & Kritik*, 01, 49–79.

26 European Social Survey 2017, http:// www.euro peansocial survey.org

27 It contained this definition of basic income: 'The government pays everyone a monthly income to cover essential living costs. It replaces many other social benefits'. European Social Survey (2017).

28 The campaign aimed at a level of €2,250 per month compared with the €800–1,200 range commonly discussed. The partial basic income versions considered in Finland at the time comprised a range between €550 and €750 per month.

29 Ford, M., 2015, *The Rise of the Robots*, London: Oneworld.

30 Cruddas, J. and Kibasi, T., 2016, 'A Universal Basic Mistake', *Prospect Magazine*, 16 June.

31 Titmuss, *Commitment to Welfare*, p. 134.

32 Blyth, M., 2013, *Austerity: The History of a Dangerous Idea*, Oxford: Oxford University Press, p. x.

33 Ibid., p. 134.

34 Standing, G., 2017, *Basic Income*, Harmondsworth: Penguin.

35 Van Parijs, P. and Vanderborght, Y., 2017, *Basic Income*, Cambridge, MA: Harvard University Press.

36 Haagh, L., 2007, 'Developmental Freedom and Social Order', *Journal of Philosophical Economics*, 1 (1), 119–60.

37 Macpherson, C.B., 1973, *Democratic Theory*, Oxford: Oxford University Press.

38 On how more stable property is hybrid, see Chang, H.J., 2011, 'Institutions and Economic Development', *Journal of Institutional Economics*, 7 (4), 473–98.

39 Sen, A., 1998, *Development as Freedom*, Oxford: Oxford University Press, chs 1 and 2.

40 Sen, A., 1987, *The Standard of Living*, Cambridge: Cambridge University Press, pp. 19–37. Sen, A., 1992, *Inequality Re-examined*, Oxford: Clarendon Press, pp. 40–2.

41 Nussbaum, M.C., 2006, *Frontiers of Justice*, Cambridge, MA: The Belknap Press, pp. 76–7.

42 Sen, A., 1985, 'Well-Being, Agency and Freedom: The Dewey Lectures 1984', *Journal of Philosophy*, 82 (4), 169–221, 203–4: and Sen, *Inequality Re-examined*, p. 40.

43 Titmuss, R.M., 1965, 'The Role of Redistribution in Social Policy', *Social Security Bulletin*, June, p. 15.

44 Pempel, T.J., 1999, 'The Developmental Regime in a Changing World Economy', in M. Woo-Cumings M. (ed.), *The Development State*, Ithaca, NY: Cornell University Press, pp. 137–81.

45 Titmuss, 'The Role of Redistribution in Social Policy', p. 15.

46 Ruggie, J.G., 1982, 'International Regimes, Transactions, and Change', *International Organization*, 36 (2), 379–415.

47 Esping-Andersen, G., 1990, *The Three Worlds of Welfare Capitalism*, Cambridge: Polity, p. 199.

48 Milanovic, B., 2016, *Global Inequality*, Cambridge, MA: Harvard University Press, pp. 74–5.

49 https://www.bbc.co.uk/news/education-37246632

50 OECD, 2015, *In It Together: Why Less Inequality Benefits All*, Paris: OECD.

51 Pyper, D. and Powell, A. 2018, 'Zero Hours Contracts', House of Commons Briefing Paper, Number 06553, 22 May, p. 29.

52 Kalleberg, A.L., 2018, *Precarious Lives*, Cambridge: Polity, 90–103, 87.

53 In the UK case, 'Larger companies are more likely to use zero-hours contracts, with 23% of workplaces that have 100 or more employees using them in 2011'. Pyper, D. and Harari, D., 2013, House of Commons Library, Standard Note: SN/BT/6553: https://fullfact.org/sites/fullfact.org/files/SN06553. pdf, p. 4.

54 OECD Employment Outlook, various years; Haagh, 'The Developmental Social Contract'.

55 Pennycook, M., Cory, G. and Alakeson, G. 2013, 'A Matter of Time: The Rise of Zero-Hours Contracts', Resolution Foundation, available at https://www. resolutionfoundation.org/app/uploads/2014/08/A_ Matter_of_Time_-_The_rise_of_zero-hours_con tracts_final_1.pdf, p. 15.

56 Ibid., pp. 16–17.

57 For a good discussion of experiments conducted in the US in the 1970s, see Widerquist, K., 2005, 'A Failure to Communicate: What (if Anything) Can We Learn from the Negative Income Tax Experiments?', *Journal of Socio-economics*, 34 (1), 49–81.

58 OECD Employment Outlook 2013, 178–83.
59 Venn, D., 2012, 'Eligibility Criteria for Unemployment Benefits', OECD Social, Employment and Migration Working Papers, No. 131, OECD Publishing, pp. 19–20.
60 National Audit Office, Benefit Sanctions, 2016.
61 Københavns Kommune 2010, Dokumentnr. 2010-840990.
62 Philip, U.N. and Sørensen, L., 2016, Analyse: Effekt af at få en sankion for ledige i kontanthjælpsystemet, November.
63 OECD Employment Outlook 2012, pp. 68–70.
64 Knotz, C.M., 2018, 'A Rising Workfare State?', *Journal of International and Comparative Social Policy*, 34 (2), 99–108, p. 105
65 Ibid., p. 106.
66 Watts, B., Fitzpatrick, S. Bramley, G. and Watkins, D., 2014, 'Welfare Sanctions and Conditionality in the UK', Joseph Rowntree Trust, available at https://www.jrf.org.uk/sites/default/files/jrf/migrated/files/Welfare-conditionality-UK-Summary.pdf; Reeves, A., 2017, 'Does Sanctioning Disabled Claimants of Unemployment Insurance Increase Labour Market Activity?', *Journal of Poverty and Social Justice*, 25 (2), 129–46.
67 Loopstra, R., Reeves, A., McKee, M. and Stuckler, D., 2015, 'Do Punitive Approaches to Unemployment Benefit Recipients Increase Welfare Exit and Employment?', University of Oxford, Sociology Working Paper, no. 2015-1.

68 The Money Charity estimates that the number of unemployed entitled to claim public funds, who do so, fell from 69% in 2000, to 60% in 2012, and to 34% in November 2016. The Money Charity, 2016, http://themoneycharity.org.uk/money-statistics/

69 National Audit Office, Benefit Sanctions, 6.

70 Sanctions were justified on the basis of claims that on average zero-hour contracts provide 25 hours of work. https://www.bbc.co.uk/news/uk-272 89148

71 Crisis, 2017, The Homeless Monitor: England 2017, pp. x–xi, 18.

72 Ibid., pp. 41, 38–45. The Office for National Statistics figures for 2017 reported a 24% increase in deaths among homeless people in five years, rising to just under 600 people, with average ages of 42 years for women, and 44 years for men. https://www.theguardian.com/society/2018/dec/20/ homeless-deaths-rise-by-a-quarter-in-five-years-official-figures-show

73 Mortality statistics: ESA, IB and SDA claimants, Department of Work and Pensions 2015, p. 5. https://www.gov.uk/government/statistics/mor tality-statistics-esa-ib-and-sda-claimants.

74 Titmuss, *Commitment to Welfare*, p. 67.

75 A New Economics Foundation Report proposal endorsed by the Shadow Chancellor of British Labour Party, released in March 2019, involves turning the tax-free allowance into a personal allowance – a decided step to a basic income, by in effect ensuring a majority in society receive

unconditional income whether earning or not. New Economics Foundation, 'Scrap Personal Allowance and Replace with a New Weekly Cash Payment', 11 March, https://neweconomics.org/2019/03/scrap-personal-allowance-and-replace-with-a-new-weekly-cash-payment. On the other hand, seeking to work a redistributive outcome through this system, without raising tax progressively, to retain fiscal neutrality, similarly to the CBIT model, has the effect of penalising high earners rather than the highest incomes or wealth, making what could be an inclusive institutional change a monetary trade-off within the labour market between low and high-skill groups. Moreover, in this case restricting the allowance to those earning less than 125,000 per annum – justified in the interest of fiscal neutrality – fails to generate a key benefit of basic income, which is to re-establish genuinely common rights. Working redistribution through a more progressive design of the tax system at the high end therefore would have been a preferable option. The difficulty in finding a transition to income benefit reform that is cost-neutral and universal at the same time, without generating crude distributive trade-offs in the labour market, illustrates the difficulty of envisaging basic income as a single distributive measure, and the more attractive routes connected with more gradual transitions combined with more ambitious fiscal reforms.

76 IMF, 2017, Fiscal Monitor, October, p. ix.

77 The case has been made for basic income as needed in replacement of the postwar order of 'stable posi-

tions'. Van der Veen, R. and Van Parijs, P., 2006, 'A Capitalist Road to Communism', *Basic Income Studies*, 1 (1), 1–23.

78 In referring to public services, Van Parijs could not find 'a principled way' to defend them (1995, *Real Freedom for All*, Oxford: Oxford University Press, p. 231), preferring – as far as possible – strict equality (ibid., pp. 21, 37) over a welfarist approach that provide according to need.

79 Murray, *In Our Hands*.

80 Van der Veen, R. and Van Parijs, P., 1986, 'A Capitalist Road to Communism', *Theory and Society*, 15 (5), 635–55.

81 Van Parijs, P., 2009, 'Egalitarian Justice, Left Libertarianism, and the Market', in I. Carter, S. de Wijze, and M. Kramer (eds), *The Anatomy of Justice*, London: Routledge, pp. 145–62, 159–60.

82 http://citizensincome.org/news/10000-for-25-year-olds/

83 Ackerman, B., Alstott, A. and van Parijs, P., 2005, *Redesigning Distribution*, London: Verso.

84 Zygmunt Bauman warned about these effects. See Bauman, Z., 1999, *In Search of Politics*, Cambridge: Polity, pp. 185–6.

85 IMF, Fiscal Monitor, pp. x, 17–21.

86 IMF, Fiscal Monitor, p. 10. Even when the IMF acknowledges the way means-testing acts as a disincentive, 'Careful attention to the design of means-tested programs is ... required to minimize work disincentives if benefits are withdrawn quickly as income rises' (p. 15).

87 Van Parijs, *Real Freedom for All*, pp. 33, 89–96.

88 Maximizing a BI's role in distributive terms formally reduces other forms of distribution – or welfare finance – to conditions everyone else would reject (Van Parijs, *Real Freedom for All*, p. 79).

89 On these grounds, Van Parijs has questioned the good of publicly providing 'expensive heart operations or cancer treatments at an advanced age' (ibid., p. 44).

90 A position restated in Van Parijs and Vanderborght, *Basic Income*, pp. 27, 29–50, which also stresses the role of basic income in safeguarding public neutrality – essentially non-intervention (p. 99).

91 Haagh, L., 2011, 'Basic Income, Social Democracy and Control over Time', *Policy & Politics*, 39 (1), 43–66.

92 Van Parijs is ambivalent about taxing superior talent (*Real Freedom for All*, p. 124), and worries that needs-based policies stigmatize per se (*Real Freedom for All*, p. 120). He is sympathetic to Dworkin's view that each life deserves the same resources (*Real Freedom for All*, p. 262).

93 https://www.theguardian.com/society/2016/may/11/force-workers-universal-credit-take-second-jobs-risky

94 In 2016, Britain had the highest share of spending on tax credits in the OECD, at 1.6% in GDP, up from 0.4% in 2000. In Nordic countries spending is minimal or not recorded (OECD tax revenue).

95 Arthur, B.W., 1994, *Increasing Returns and Path Dependence in the Economy*. Ann Arbor, MI: University of Michigan Press.

Chapter 2: Human Development Freedom

1 Marshall, T.H., 1950, *Citizenship and Social Class*, Cambridge: Cambridge University Press, pp. 64–5.
2 Fromm, E., 1966, 'The Psychological Aspects of the Guaranteed Income', in R. Theobald (ed.), *The Guaranteed Income: Next Step in Economic Evolution?* New York: Doubleday and Co., pp. 175–84.
3 Fromm, E., 1994, *On Being Human*, New York: Continuum, p. 35.
4 For example, Ravallion, M., 2003, 'Targeted Transfers in Poor Countries', SPDP Series No. 0314, The World Bank; and Ravallion, M., 2017, 'Inequality and Globalisation: A Review Essay', Society for the Study of Economic Inequality, ECINEQ WP 2017-435.
5 Moore, C., 2008, *Assessing Honduras' CCT Programme PRAF*, International Poverty Centre Country Study, 15, Brasília.
6 Hirschman, A.O., 1991, *The Rhetoric of Reaction*, Cambridge, MA: Harvard University Press.
7 Hayek, F.A., 1980, *1980s Unemployment and the Unions*, London: Institute of Economic Affairs.
8 Mead, L. (ed.), 1997, *The New Paternalism*, Washington, DC: Brookings Institution Press.

9 Ibid., p. 177.

10 Ibid., p. 167.

11 Main, T.J., 1997, 'Homeless Men in New York City: Toward Paternalism through Privatization', in L. Mead, *The New Paternalism*, Washington, DC: Brookings Institution Press, p. 167.

12 Ibid., p. 174.

13 Ibid.

14 Ibid., p. 175.

15 Van Parijs guards against justifying more resources to those living longer on a humanist principle: rather, the justification is that we are not the same person at different ages (Van Parijs, *Real Freedom for All*, p. 46). Our right to expensive treatment diminishes with age (ibid., p. 44).

16 Ravallion, 'Inequality and Globalisation', pp. 19–20.

17 Ibid., p. 20.

18 Lavinas, L., 2018, 'The Collateralization of Social Policy under Financialized Capitalism', *Development and Change*, 49 (2), 502–17.

19 Sen, *Inequality Re-examined*, pp. 46–8, 53, 72; Robeyns, I., 2016, 'The Capability Approach', Stanford, CA: Stanford Encyclopedia of Philosophy, https : / / plato . stanford . edu / entries / capability - approach/ 3.1, is a good summary.

20 Nussbaum, *Frontiers of Justice*, pp. 76–7.

21 'Moving all citizens above a basic threshold of capability should be taken as a central social goal. When citizens are across the threshold, societies are to a greater extent free to choose the other goals they wish to pursue' (Nussbaum, M., 1999, *Sex*

and Social Justice, Oxford: Oxford University Press, pp. 42–3, emphasis added).

22 Nussbaum's equivalence is evident in her doubt as to how to settle the question whether Amish communities' way of life overrides young people's interest in longer schooling and gender equality. Nussbaum, M., 2000, *Women and Human Development*, Cambridge: Cambridge University Press, p. 233.

23 Sen, *The Standard of Living*, pp. 19, 37.

24 Marshall, *Citizenship and Social Class*, p. 35.

25 Robeyns, 'The Capability Approach', 2.2.

26 Haagh, 'Developmental Freedom and Social Order', pp. 119–60.

27 Archer, R., 2007, *Why Is There No Labour Party in the United States?* Princeton, NJ: Princeton University Press.

28 Jayadev, A. and Bowles, S., 2006, 'Guard Labour', *Journal of Development Economics*, 79 (2), 328–48.

29 Thelen, K., 2014, *Varieties of Liberalization*, Cambridge: Cambridge University Press, pp. 124–5.

30 Haagh, L., 2012, 'Democracy, Public Finance, and Property Rights in Economic Stability', *Polity*, 44 (4), 542–87.

31 Kahneman, D., 2011, *Thinking, Fast and Slow*, Harmondsworth: Penguin; Callard, F., Smallwood, J., Golchert, J. and Margulies, D.S., 2013, 'The Era of the Wandering Mind?', *Frontiers in Psychology*, 4, 891.

32 Forget, E., 2011, 'A Town with No Poverty', *Canadian Public Policy*, 37 (3), 283–305.

33 Ibid.; Ruckert, A., Huynh, C. and Labonté, R., 2017, 'Reducing Health Inequities', *Journal of Public Health*, 40 (1), 3–7.

34 Haagh, 'Working Life, Well-Being and Welfare Reform'.

35 Samuels, F. and Stavropoulou, M., 2016, 'Being Able to Breathe Again', *Journal of Development Studies*, 52 (8), 1099–114.

36 Cantor, N. and Sanderson, C.A., 2003, 'Life-Task Participation and Wellbeing', in D. Kahneman, E. Diener and N. Schwarz (eds), *Well-Being: The Foundations of Hedonic Psychology*, New York: Russell Sage Foundation.

37 Peterson, C., 2003, 'Personal Control and Well-Being', in D. Kahneman et al., *Well-Being*, pp. 291–2.

38 A tragic case in point is that of a young man who committed suicide when the motorcycle he used to work as a courier was seized in relation to a parking fine which had escalated from £65 to £1,019. https://www.theguardian.com/money/2017/apr/30/debt - ridden - couriers - suicide - after - bailiff - visit - prompts-call-for-reforms

39 Having to prove vulnerability to access support can damage health, as illustrated by the case of poor HIV sufferers in South Africa, who stopped taking medicines to access disability grants. Natrass, N., 2005, 'AIDS, Disability and the Case for a Basic Income Grant in South Africa'. http://www.avinus-magazin.eu/2005/11/18/nattrass-aids-grundeinkommen/

40 https://www.youtube.com/watch?v=G2lNRxIcfQo

41 Quoted in Williams, E., 2014, 'A Fast Guide to Zero Hours Contracts in the NHS', *Health Services Journal*, 20 January, p. 3.

42 Sanctions decisions are also delayed. According to the auditor (National Audit Office, Benefit Sanctions, 8), in August 2016 nearly half (42%) of decisions about sanctions within the unified new Universal Credit system took more than 28 days to decide.

43 https://www.instituteforgovernment.org.uk/blog/problems-universal-credit, submitted by Coping mum (not verified) on Wed, 2017-09-20, 14:46.

44 Rawls, J., 1971, *A Theory of Justice*, Oxford: Oxford University Press, p. 378.

45 North, D.C., 2005, *Understanding the Process of Economic Change*, Princeton, NJ: Princeton University Press, pp. 14–15.

46 Tatsiramos, K., 2009, 'Unemployment Insurance in Europe', *Journal of the European Economic Association*, 7 (6), 1225–60.

47 Haagh, 'Working Life, Well-Being and Welfare Reform'.

48 Fredrickson, B. et al., 2013, 'A Functional Genomic Perspective on Human Well-Being', *Proceedings of the National Academy of Sciences of the United States of America*, 110 (33), 13684–9.

49 Cantor and Sanderson, 'Life-Task Participation and Wellbeing', pp. 232–3.

50 Sennett, R., 2008, *The Craftsman*, London: Penguin Books, pp. 54–6, 63.

51 Hood, B., 2014, *The Domesticated Brain*, London: Penguin Books, pp. 134–5, 193, 203–4, 267–8.

52 Hudson, V. and Matfess, H., 2017, 'In Plain Sight', *International Security*, 42 (1), 7–40.

53 Widerquist, K., 2013, *Independence, Property-lessness, and Basic Income*, Basingstoke: Palgrave. Hirschman, A., 1970, *Exit, Voice, and Loyalty*, Cambridge, MA: Harvard University Press.

54 Sen, A., 1987, 'Gender and Cooperative Conflicts', Wider Working Papers 18, July, 20–1.

55 Ibid., p. 27.

56 Haagh, 'Working Life, Well-Being and Welfare Reform', pp. 462–5.

57 The Resolution Foundation finds 91% of persons with the same employer experienced fluctuations in income in 2016–17 (5), with an average of 10% fluctuations across those surveyed. Their findings that fluctuations are concentrated at the higher and lower end of the earnings spectrum can be hypothesized to reflect, respectively, the greater uncertainty around work schedules, and greater performance-related pay structures, for these two groups. Eighty percent of lower earners, defined as taking home around 10,000 p.a., experienced volatile pay. See https://www.resolutionfoundation.org/app/uploads/2018/10/Irregular-payments-RF-REPORT.pdf

58 Cecchini, S. and Martínez, R., 2012, 'Inclusive Social Protection in Latin America', Economic Commission for Latin America, Santiago, Chile, pp. 107–8, 112–13.

59 Clair, A., Reeves, A., Loopstra, R., McKee, M., Dorling, D. and Stuckler, D., 2016, 'The Impact of the Housing Crisis on Self-Reported Health in

Europe', *European Journal of Public Health*, 26 (5), 788–93.

60 This information was obtained in conversations with a public defence lawyer in Guernsey, in July 2017.

61 Standing, G., 2002, *Beyond the New Paternalism*, London: Verso; Haagh, 'Basic Income, Social Democracy and Control over Time'.

62 Goodin, R.E., Rice, J.M., Parpo, A. and Eriksson, L., 2008, *Discretionary Time: A New Measure of Freedom*, Cambridge: Cambridge University Press; Goodin, R.E., 2001, 'Work and Welfare', *British Journal of Political Science*, 31, 13–39.

63 Based on the Fifth European Survey on Working Conditions, 2010.

64 Steinmo, S., 2010, *The Evolution of Modern States*, Cambridge: Cambridge University Press, pp. 72–3; Haagh, 'Democracy, Public Finance, and Property Rights'.

65 In Denmark, direct subsidy of privately governed schools to a level of between 85% and 100% of their costs ensures the level of fees is contained. See Haagh, L., 2015. 'Alternative Social States and the Basic Income Debate', *Basic Income Studies*, 10 (1), 45–81.

66 Haagh, 'Alternative Social States'.

67 Haagh, L., 2001, 'The Challenges of Labor Reform in Korea', in F. Park et al. (eds), *Labor Market Reforms in Korea*, Washington, DC: The World Bank.

68 Piketty, T., 2013, *Capital in the Twenty-First Century*, Cambridge, MA: Harvard University Press, pp. 315, 34.

69 Appendix Table A4ii, Column 11.

70 Haagh, 'Alternative Social States', 67.

71 The Supreme Court 2017, Judgment, *UNISON v Lord Chancellor*, https://www.supremecourt.uk/cases/uksc-2015-0233.html, p. 4.

72 According to the summary of the Supreme Court, 'the main purpose of a fee structure was to transfer part of the cost burden from the tax payer to the users of the service, since a significant majority of the population would never use ETs' (ibid.).

73 The representation made in the Supreme Court case supported 'the view of commentators … that some employers were delaying negotiations to see whether the claimant would be prepared to pay the fee' (ibid., p. 18).

74 http://www.bbc.co.uk/news/uk-40727400

75 https://www.lawgazette.co.uk/law/supreme-court-humiliates-government-over-tribunal-fees/5062220.article

76 Summary of the judgment of the Divisional Court (Lord Justice Singh and Mr Justice Lewis) 11 January 2019 In R (on the application of (1) Danielle Johnson (2) Claire Woods (3) Erin Barrett and (4) Katie Stewart) v Secretary of State for Work and Pensions, https://www.judiciary.uk/wp-content/uploads/2019/01/johnson-dwp-summary.pdf

77 Universal credit: Single mums win High Court battle: https://www.bbc.co.uk/news/uk-46834533

Chapter 3: Democratic Development

1 Spence, 'The Real Rights of Man'.
2 Paine, *Agrarian Justice*, p. 32.
3 Appendix Table A1.
4 Oxfam estimates that global corporate investment in tax havens quadrupled between 2001 and 2014. Oxfam, 2017, 'Paradise Papers: The Hidden Costs of Tax Dodging', p. 5.
5 Sahay, R. et al., 2015, 'Rethinking Financial Deepening', IMF SDN/15/08, pp. 10–11.
6 Shaxson, N., 'The UK's Shadow Economy: £40 billion Lost to Treasury', Tax Justice Network, 20 May 2014.
7 Citizens' Basic Income Trust, 2018, Basic Income – a Brief Introduction, p. 8.
8 For a short but concise critique, see https://www.the guardian.com/global/shortcuts/2017/oct/29/how-the-actual-magic-money-tree-works
9 https://www.independent.co.uk/news/business/news/private-landlords-taxpayer-money-housing-benefits-rent-housing-crisis-low-income-families-a7199111.html
10 The British social housing bill is much larger than in comparator countries where rent controls enable the public to save. In 2014, housing benefit spend in Denmark represented 5.3% (at DKK70 million) of combined housing and income transfer spend (on families, housing, income, unemployment and sickness benefits) (Statistisk Årbog, 2016, 68). In comparison, in the UK, housing benefit represented

181

24% (£26 billion) of the above posts (at about £132 billion) in 2015/6 (Department of Work and Pensions, Annual Report 2015/16).

11 IMF, 2017, Fiscal Monitor, October, p. ix.

12 Ibid., p. 12.

13 Ibid., p. 13

14 McKinsey Global Institute, 2012, 'The World at Work', pp. 2, 3.

15 Góes, C. and Karpowicz, I., 2017, 'Inequality in Brazil', IMF Working Paper WP/17/225, p. 3.

16 Oxfam, 2016, *An Economy for the 1%*, Oxford: Oxfam, p. 10.

17 World Bank, 2017, 'Reducing Inequality in the State of Bahia, Brazil', 17 April.

18 Góes and Karpowicz, 'Inequality in Brazil', p. 19.

19 As noted in chapter 1. Table A1, Columns 6b and 8b, show the multiples of income at which higher rates of tax set in, and trend.

20 The data are shown in Table A3 in the Appendix.

21 Table A4 in the Appendix.

22 The occupational citizenship concept was first explored in Haagh, L., 2002, *Citizenship, Labour Markets, and Democratization – Chile and the Modern Sequence*, New York: Palgrave, and Haagh, L., 1999, 'Training Policy and the Property Rights of Labour in Chile (1990–1997): Social Citizenship in the Atomised Market Regime', *Journal of Latin American Studies*, 31, 429–72.

23 Bramley, G., Hirsch, D., Littlewood, M. and Watkins, D., 2016, 'Counting the Cost of Poverty',

Joseph Rowntree Foundation, available at https://www.jrf.org.uk/report/counting-cost-uk-poverty, pp. 22, 4.

24 For a single person over 25 it was about DKK7,800 per month in 2013 after tax (Bjørn, N.H. and Høj, A.K., 2014, 'Understøttelse ved ledighed in syv lande', *Det Økonomiske Råds Sekretariat*, 2014:2, 23–4), compared with the equivalent of about DKK2,756 in Britain, not counting housing support in either case.

25 Byrd, B.S. and Hrushschka, J., 2005, 'Kant on Why Must I Keep My Promise', *Chicago-Kent Law Review*, 81 (5), 47–74, p. 49.

26 Whitehead, L., 2002, *Democratization*, Oxford: Oxford University Press, p. 167.

27 Dahrendorf, R., 1959, *Class and Class Conflict in Industrial Society*, Stanford, CA: Stanford University Press.

28 Durkheim, E., 1960 [1893]. *The Division of Labor in Society*, New York: The Free Press, p. 5.

29 Almost one-third of households in the UK were single-occupant in 2013, up from about 20% in 1981 (https://visual.ons.gov.uk/uk-perspectives-housing-and-home-ownership-in-the-uk/). One in eight elderly were found to have unmet everyday needs due to absence of care. Mortimer, J. and Green, M., 2015, 'Briefing: The Health and Care of Older People in England', Age UK, available at http://www.cpa.org.uk/cpa/docs/AgeUK-Briefing-The HealthandCareofOlderPeopleinEngland-2015.pdf, p. 5.

30 The UK charity Crisis estimates that deaths resulting from homelessness doubled between 2012 and 2017, https://www.theguardian.com/society/2018/apr/11/deaths-of-uk-homeless-people-more-than-double-in-five-years, p. 21.

31 James, D., 2012, 'Conceptual Innovation in Fichte's Theory of Property', *European Journal of Philosophy*, 23 (3), 509–28, 517–18.

32 Hence 'property rights in stability' is a modern problem for justice. Haagh, 'Democracy, Public Finance, and Property Rights'.

33 Urs Rohner, Credit Suisse Chairman, cited in *Guardian*, 'Richest 1% own half the world's wealth, study finds', 14 November 2017.

34 According to research by Prudential, between 2016 and 2018, the level of pensioner debt rose by 80% in the UK, with one in five pensioners affected, and their debt averaging £33,900. https://www.professionaladviser.com/professional-adviser/news/3025856/pensioner-debt-jumps-80-in-two-years-to-average-gbp33-900

35 McKinsey, 'The World at Work', p. 2.

36 http://www.undp.org/content/undp/en/home/mdgoverview/post-2015-development-agenda.html

37 See further https://www.mein-grundeinkommen.de/infos/in-english

38 Conversations with leading members of the campaign group MeinGrundincommen, at the websummit in Lisbon on 6 November 2017.

39 Conversations with a backer of the new cryptocurrency EOS, which formally launched in June

2018. EOS is a third-generation cryptocurrency (CC), following Bitcoin, which was created in 2008, and Etherium, which was released in 2013. EOS, like the previous CCs, is based on computer algorithms. Investors buy currency tokens at a set value. Etherium set up smart contracts to regulate transaction relationships. EOS is seeking to generate formal arbitration boards.

40 According to one estimate, the value of Etherium grew more than 11-fold between April 2017, when its value stood at around $50 per token, and the end of the year, when it had risen to $730. https://globalcoin report.com/current-eos-consistency-might-be-the-start-of-something-extraordinary/

41 A debate is ongoing within EOS about governance: should votes be based on the size of investments, or one-wallet (or account) one-vote, as currently? A splinter group calling itself EOS evolution prefers the democratic formula.

42 As an investor in Etherium, interviewed in April 2018, noted, the value of cryptocurrencies is always deeply affected by political crises, such as in Zimbabwe and the Syrian crisis, when states fail and citizens lose a foothold in political communities.

43 Arendt, H. 1958, *The Human Condition*, Chicago, IL: Chicago University Press, p. 52.

44 Le Roux, P., 2006, Session 'Poverty and Its Remedies in South Africa', BIEN Congress, Cape Town, 3 November.

45 Dutrey, A.P., 2007, 'Successful Targeting? Reporting Efficiency and Costs in Targeted Poverty

Alleviation Programmes', UNRISD, SPDPP No. 35, November, p. 9.

46 Cornia, A. and Stewart, F., 1993, 'Two Errors of Targeting', *Journal of International Development*, 5 (5), 459–96.

47 Interview with Ana Fonseca, head of fielding cash grants, São Paulo municipality, July 2005.

48 Nistotskaya, M. and D'Arcy, M., 2018, 'Getting to Sweden', in S.H. Steinmo (ed.), *The Leap of Faith*, Oxford: Oxford University Press, pp. 33–55.

49 Kananen, J., 2014, *The Nordic Welfare State in Three Eras*, Farnham: Ashgate; Haagh, L., 2019, 'Public Ownership within Varieties of Capitalism: Regulatory Foundations for Welfare and Freedom', *International Journal of Public Policy*, Special Issue on Public Ownership in the Twenty-First Century, A. Cummine and S. White (eds), forthcoming.

50 Kohli, A., 1994, 'Where Do High Growth Political Economies Come From?', *World Development*, 22 (9), 1269–93.

51 Nayyar, D., 1998, 'Economic Development and Political Democracy', *Economic and Political Weekly*, 33 (49), 3121–31.

52 Haagh, L., 2002, 'The Emperor's New Clothes: Labor Reform and Social Democratization in Chile', *Studies in Comparative International Development*, 37 (1), 86–115.

53 Pettit, P., 2013, 'Two Republican Traditions', in A. Niederberger and P. Schink (eds), *Republican Democracy: Liberty, Law and Politics*, Edinburgh: Edinburgh University Press, pp. 169–204.

54 Ibid., citing Paley 1825, 168.
55 Thelen, *Varieties of Liberalization*; Finegold, D. and Soskice, D., 1988, 'The Failure of Training in Britain: Analysis and Prescription', *Oxford Economic Review*, 4 (3), 21–53.
56 Sandberg, L.G., 1979, 'The Case of the Impoverished Sophisticate: Human Capital and Swedish Economic Growth before World War I', *Journal of Economic History*, 39 (1), 225–41.
57 Sandberg, L.G., 1978, 'Banking and Economic Growth in Sweden before World War I', *Journal of Economic History*, 38 (3), 650–80.
58 Forget, E., 2017, 'Do We Still Need a Basic Income Guarantee in Canada?', http://www.northernpolicy. ca/dowestillneedabig
59 https://www.nao.org.uk/wp-content/uploads/2018/ 06/Rolling-out-Universal-Credit.pdf, pp. 58–60.
60 Davala, S. 2018., 'The Indian Experience: The Debt Trap and the Unconditional Basic Income', in A. Downes and S. Lansley (eds), *It's Basic Income*, Bristol: Policy Press, pp. 136–40.
61 In 2016, I suggested thinking in terms of Basic Income Plus, to address the impression basic income requires replacement of existing welfare services and means- or needs-based transfers. Haagh, L., Danish Parliament, Christiansborg – Basic Income and the Nordic Model – September 2016: https://www.you tube.com/watch?v=YsDyzrE9csw. Elder-Woodward and Duffy, focusing on disability, have used a simi- lar term in a British context; see Elder-Woodward, J. and Duffy, S. 2018, 'An Emancipatory Welfare

State', https://www.citizen-network.org/wp-content/uploads/An-Emancipatory-Welfare-State.pdf

62 Korpi, W. and Palme, J., 1998, 'The Paradox of Redistribution and Strategies of Equality', *American Sociological Review*, 63 (5), 661–87.

63 Svalfors, S., 2012, *Contested Welfare States*, Stanford, CA: Stanford University Press, p. 208.

64 Attitudes towards equality are more 'integrated' (coherent across dimensions) in Sweden compared with Germany and especially Anglo-liberal countries. Svallfors, S., 2006, *The Moral Economy of Class: Class and Attitudes in Comparative Perspective*, Stanford, CA: Stanford University Press, pp. 69, 163; Svallfors, S., 2007, 'Class and Attitudes to Market Inequality', in S. Svallfors (ed.), *The Political Sociology of the Welfare State*, Stanford, CA: Stanford University Press, pp. 216–17.

65 Portes et al. suggest basic services as an alternative to monetary redistribution and UBI (Portes, J. et al., 2017, 'Social Prosperity for the Future', Institute for Global Prosperity, University College London, pp. 6, 13).

66 Coyle, D., 2017, 'How to Have a Productive Brexit', *Prospect Magazine*, 13 November.

67 Ibid.

68 Portes et al., 'Social Prosperity for the Future', pp. 41–2.

69 Ibid., pp. 13–14.

70 Atkinson, T. and Weale, M., 2000, 'James Edward Meade 1907–1995', *Proceedings of the British Academy*, 105, 473–500, p. 493.

71 Ibid., 485.
72 https://www.gainhealth.org/knowledge-centre/fast-facts-malnutrition/
73 https://www.theguardian.com/global-development-professionals-network/2017/mar/17/access-to-drinking-water-world-six-infographics
74 Such as by the Danish painter Hohlenberg; translated in Birnbaum, S. and Christensen, E., 2007, 'Anthroposophical Reflections on Basic Income', *Basic Income Studies*, 2 (2), 1–17.
75 Ford, *The Rise of the Robots*.
76 Esping-Andersen, G., *The Three Worlds of Welfare Capitalism*, p. 199.
77 https://basicincome.org/news/2018/06/the-future-of-abundance-self-owning-machines-can-generate-a-basic-income/
78 Pagano, U., 2017, Why Have Only Humans and Social Insects Evolved a Complex Division of Labor', Quaderni dipartimento di Economia politica, Università di Siena No. 768.
79 Briône, P., 2017, 'Mind over Machines: New Technology and Employment Relations', Acas, http://www.acas.org.uk/media/pdf/i/9/Minds-over-Machines-New-Technology-and-Employment-Relations.pdf
80 In a single month (March 2017) the NHS posted 30,613 full-time equivalent vacancies. Mundasad, S., 2017, 'More than 86,000 NHS posts vacant, says report', BBC News, 25 July.
81 https://www.opendemocracy.net/neweconomics/preston-model-modern-politics-municipal-socialism/

82 https://www.wsj.com/articles/how-bad-is-the-labor-shortage-cities-will-pay-you-to-move-there-1525102030

83 Van den Berg, L., Hebinck, P. and Roep, D., 2018, 'We Go Back to the Land', *Journal of Peasant Studies*, 45 (3), 653–75.

84 https://www.kristeligt-dagblad.dk/historier/drejoe

85 https://www.wired.com/story/free-money-the-surprising-effects-of-a-basic-income-supplied-by-government/

86 Standing, G. and Samson, M., 2003, *A Basic Income Grant for South Africa*, Cape Town: UCT Press.

87 Suplicy, E., 2002, *Renda da Cidadania*, São Paulo: Cortez Editora.

88 Davala, S., Jhabvala, R., Standing, G. and Mehta, S.K., 2015, *Basic Income: A Transformative Policy for India*, London: Bloomsbury.

89 The Danish system covers 100% of average salary, but 88% for those (previously) earning two-thirds of the average wage. For the UK, the rates are 28% and 33%. Bjørn and Høj, 'Understøttelse ved ledighed in syv lande', pp. 27–8.

90 Without tax subsidy, premiums on lower earners would have the effect of excluding them (Bjørn and Høj, 'Understøttelse ved ledighed in syv lande', p. 10).

91 Ibid., pp. 9–20.

92 Arbejdesmarkedstyrelsen, Beskætigelsesudvalget 2012–13, BEU alm. Del Bilag 19.

93 Parg 13 of LBK nr, 190 of 24.02.2012, Lov om Aktiv Socialpolitik.

94 Haagh, 'Public Ownership within Varieties of Capitalism'.

95 Caswell, D., et al., 2011, 'Når Kassen Smækkes I', AKF Rapport, November, p. 10.

96 Calculation is in Haagh, 'The Developmental Social Contract'.

97 Philip, U.N. and Sørensen, L., 2016, *Analyse Effekt af at få en Sanktion for Ledige i Kontanthjælpssystemet*, Copenhagen: Beskæftigelsesministeriet.

98 Solas, S., 2018, Social worker, testimony given on the occasion of the 'Basic Income in Danish conference', Christiansborg, 15 March.

99 Interviews, Aarhus municipality, 8 December 2016.

100 For a critique of flexicurity as a route to basic income, see Haagh, 'The Developmental Social Contract'.

101 Svallfors, S., 2011, 'A Bedrock of Support? Trends in Welfare State Attitudes in Sweden, 1981–2010', *Social Policy and Administration*, 45 (7), 806–25.

102 In 2017, the British Chancellor of the Exchequer had to abandon plans to raise contributions of self-employed workers: https://www.theguardian.com/politics/2017/mar/11/omnicshambles-how-it-all-went-wrong-for-spreadsheet-phil-hammond

103 Bente Sorgenfrei, the leader of the largest Danish union, FTF (450,000 members), speech in the Danish Parliament, 15 March 2018, https://www.youtube.com/watch?v=9LyLvM3yNy8

104 Hjordt Knudsen, A. et al., 2018, *Borgerløn på Dansk*, Copenhagen, pp. 21, 34, available at http://basisindkomst.dk/wp-content/uploads/2018/11/

borgerl%C3%B8n_p%C3%A5_dansk_31102018.
pdf

105 The above-cited report positions basic income as a
continuation of the flexicurity strategy, p. 21. For a
further discussion, see Haagh, 'The Developmental
Social Contract'.

106 Ringen, S., 2007, *What Democracy Is For*, Oxford:
Oxford University Press, pp. 77–8.

Conclusion

1 Marshall, *Citizenship and Social Class*, pp. 34–8.

2 Ibid., p. 18.

3 Van Parijs, P., 1996, 'Basic Income and the Two
Dilemmas of the Welfare State', *Political Quarterly*,
67 (1), 63–6.

4 Haagh, 'The Developmental Social Contract',
and Haagh, L., 2019, 'Governance Capacity and
Institutional Change: Basic Income Reform in
European Welfare States', *Social Policy and Society*,
forthcoming.

5 Haagh, 'Working Life, Well-Being and Welfare
Reform'.

6 Ministry of Social Affairs and Health, Finland, *The
Basic Income Experiment 2017–2018 in Finland: Pre-
liminary Results*. Reports and memorandums of the
Ministry of Social Affairs and Health 2019:9. Avail-
able at http://julkaisut.valtioneuvosto.fi/bitstream/
handle/10024/161361/Report_The%20Basic%20
Income%20Experiment%2020172018%20in%20
Finland.pdf?sequence=1&isAllowed=y, p.15.

Index

193

Index

Index

Index

Index

Index

trajectories 13, 16; function 68–9; and human activities 17, 36; human development approach 9, 16, 53, 58, 61; human development freedom 17, 51; and human limits 140; and humanist governance and norms 52; and humanist standards 57, 61; institutions of 9, 145; investment 117; life course 5; modalities 59–60; in Nordic states 98; opportunities to flourish 16; processes 59, 60; sheltering of 74, protective institutions 37; and public goods 45; and public services 8, 16, 23, 64, 122; public spending on and trends 101; and regulation 42; services 7; and social development 68; stable positions 35, 170; and well-being 16; *see also* human development justice

human development approach 58, 61; and choice 16
human development freedom: definition 17; rights constitutive of 65
human development justice 61, 82; and regularity principle 96
human ecology 60, 68; life course 5
human cconomy 60, 62, 77; systems of 60
human economy justice 67
human functioning 68–9; developmental underpinnings 68
human learning 73, 117; sequence-based 73
human limits 140
human security 50, 68, 148; fiscal public 50
humanist governance 52, 60–1, 68, 90
humanist justice 61, 65, 137; everyday 87
humanist norms 44, 54, 57
Huynh Chao 176n33
hybrid property 7

informalization 67, 129;
of society 7, 70
insecurity 75; *see*
economic security
institutions: cooperative
institutions 82, 120,
142; democratically
constituted 46;
developmental 59;
good institutions
143; governing of 59;
human development
protective 37; humanist
institutions 88;
inherited 65; institution-
building 3, 145; just
65; stable institutions
51; and Sustainable
Development Goals 106
interests: human 62; in
existential security 3–4
in-work benefits 29, 32–3
Ireland 25
Italy 25

James, David 104
Japan 47–8
Jayadev, Arjun 175n28
Jhabvala Renata 190n88
jobs: creation 47–8, 97;
good jobs 4; graduates

chasing 22; irregular
hours 27; joblessness 97;
low-skill 22; mass pool
22; protected jobs 82;
scarcity of 36; unstable
contracts 22; *see also*
employment
Jobseeker's Allowance 25
Joseph Rowntree
Foundation 102,
183n23
junk jobs 121
justice: check on
government 23, 87;
and deterrence 87;
process of attaining 87;
employment and equal
shares 41, 43; everyday
justice 88; humanist
60; and inequality 14;
institutions to support
justice 88; and market
contractual norms 90; to
prevail 87–8; publicness
of 85; reason for 90;
remote 90; and stability
89; strict egalitarianism
41; and wealth 85

Kahneman, Daniel
175n31, 176n36–7

Index

Index

Index

Offe, Claus 11
opportunities, formal, 64;
    individual 16
out-of-work benefits
    32–33
ownership: hybrid 15;
    traps 46; *see also*
    property
Oxfam 95, 181n4,
    182n16

Pagano, Ugo 189n78
Paine, Thomas 1, 10, 19,
    93–4, 162n2, 181n2
Palme, Joakim 117,
    188n62
para-states 105
parenting, authority
    in 71
paternalism 174n11
Pedersen, Ove 8
Pempel, T. J. 166n44
Pennycook 55; Matthew
pensions: public 10;
    pension credit 32–3
personal control: over
    daily life 69; and
    well-being 64; *see also*
    control
Peterson, C. 176n36
Pettit, Philip 186n53

Philip, Ulla N. 168n62,
    181n97
Piketty, Thomas 83,
    178n68
pivot 3–5, 147
pivoting state 4
planning: of development
    21; occupational 23;
    of working life 46;
    platform capitalism 149;
    see also capitalism
political elitism 21
poor, moral correction
    of 54
Poor Laws 20
policy complementarity
    23; and human
    development 136
populism 7
Portes, Jonathan 188n65,
    188n68
postwar: peace, welfare 19
poverty, 6, 12; alleviation
    1; anti-poverty policy
    53, 55; causes of 56;
    child poverty 6; and
    compensation 12; and
    crime 20; cumulative
    disadvantage 5; *see also*
    destitution
Powell, Andy 167n51

Index

Index

social security 108, 114;
diversification of 113,
143
social services 19; relation
with citizens 66
social welfare: baseline 35;
see also welfare, social
provision, public
society: civil society 7;
constitution 93;
constructed 51;
democratic 15; stability
of 101; fabric 7;
incorporation of 2, 13,
18, 23; informalization
27; security in 68, 108;
workless 12; *see also*
civil rights
solidarity 135
Sørensen, Louise 168n62,
191n97
South Africa 111, 123
South Korea 112, 157
Spain 2
Spence, Thomas 1, 19, 93,
162n1, 181n1
spot-purchasing 22
stability: in education 5;
in external income
security 5; employment
150; stable social

positions 35; stable
structures 68, 89; in
work structures 68, 77
standards: humanist 57,
61; public 57
standardization 54; and
competition 8–9
Standing, Guy 15,
165n34, 179n61,
190n86, 190n88
state: Anglo-liberal 49;
capacity 3; competition
state 8, 164n16;
disempowerment
of 106; as
distributive agent
20; entrepreneurial
21, 107, fiscal 9; and
informal structures
109; insurer of last
resort 115; and
libertarianism 36;
Nordic 49; parastatals
105; pivoting states 4;
protective 20; punitive
20; regulatory 84;
seventeenth-century
19; sixteenth-century
19; smaller role for
12; social democratic
50, 132

Index

of 26; schedules 113;
time profile 36–7; time
use 35; *see also* control;
work
Titmuss, Richard 10,
13–14, 19–20, 28, 79,
164n19–n20, 165n31,
166n43, 166n45,
169n74
tragedy, 69; double
tragedy, 77; tragic
choices 65
training: investment in,
117; spending, 98;
spending and trends, 49;
tax breaks, 97; *see also*
education
transformation 3
trickle-down economics 23

UK 22, 25–8, 47–8, 81,
94, 96, 99–100, 102,
111, 114, 117–18, 122,
124, 126, 129, 132,
154–6, 158–61, 167n53,
168n66, 181n6, 181n10,
183n29, 184n30,
184n34, 190n89
UN 106
uncertainty 27, 150,
178n57

unemployment 21;
systems 126–8; youth
105
unemployment insurance
99–100, 132–4
unions 21; membership
132; *see also* labour
United States 1, 157,
175n27, 177n48
Universal Basic
Infrastructure 118; and
housing 150
Universal Basic Services
118
Universal Credit 114
universal health 143; *see
also* health
universal suffrage 52
universality: basic 42; of
outcome 42
Urs, Rohner 184n33

Van den Berg, Leonardo
190n83
Van der Veen, Robert
171n77, 177n80
van Parijs, Philippe 15,
36, 41, 145, 165n35,
171n78, 171n80–1,
171n83, 172n87–90,
172n92, 174n15, 192n3

215

Index